The Wind Waits for Me

The Wind Waits for Me

The Art and Poetry of Van Dorn Hooker, III

Edited by Zelda Leah Gatuskin

SANTA FE

Photograph opposite page is from a photo by John Hooker

Sunstone books may be purchased for educational, business, or sales promotional use. For information please write: Special Markets Department, Sunstone Press, P.O. Box 2321, Santa Fe, New Mexico 87504-2321.

body typeface » LuzSans-Book
Printed on acid-free paper
∞
eBook 978-1-61139-329-3

Library of Congress Cataloging-in-Publication Data

Hooker, Van Dorn, 1921-
[Works. Selections]
The wind waits for me : the art and poetry of Van Dorn Hooker, III / edited by Zelda Leah Gatuskin.
pages cm
ISBN 978-1-63293-031-6 (softcover : alk. paper)
I. Gatuskin, Zelda Leah, editor. II. Title.
PS3558.O556A6 2014
818'.54--dc23
2014032756

WWW.SUNSTONEPRESS.COM
SUNSTONE PRESS / POST OFFICE BOX 2321 / SANTA FE, NM 87504-2321 /USA
(505) 988-4418 / ORDERS ONLY (800) 243-5644 / FAX (505) 988-1025

In memory of Van Dorn Hooker, III
9/15/1954–10/12/1976

From small notebook (3.5"x 6" page), a shared journal from 1973-74 at Earlham Collage; black ink is Van; blue ink is his friend Randy.

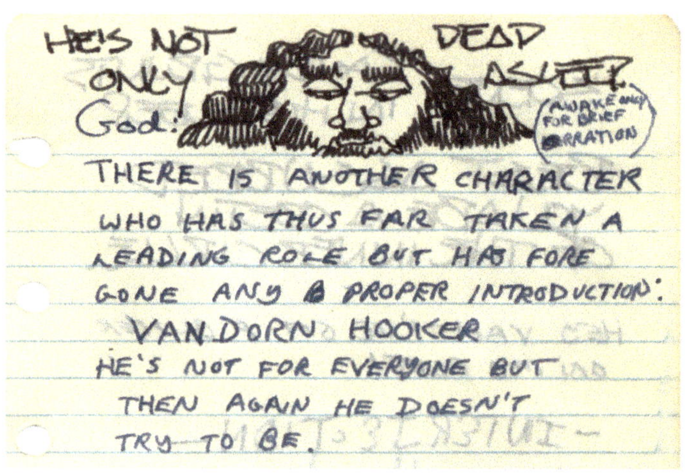

Contents

Editor's Note

The art, photography, poetry and prose on the following pages is by Van Dorn Hooker, III. For the most part, the work dates from his high school and college years, starting in about 1972 and going up to October 1976, when Van was killed in a highway accident at the age of twenty-two. It is natural to try to imagine how Van and his art might have evolved over the years, but, young as he was, Van was hardly just setting out on the path of an artist.

From the time I was shown the first batch of work, I felt this portfolio stood on its own. Even Van's casual jottings are full of perceptive wit and high graphic style. Kooky characters and sharp social commentary populate his class notes, journals, letters, and sketchbooks. The more formal works are beautifully designed and executed, demonstrating his dedication to craft. The writings often reflect the torment below the surface, a combination of despair and desire that comes with the title, Artist. Although Van's life was tragically cut short, I could not approach this collection as something unfinished or only for memorial purpose. Here is art doing what art does: making us laugh, cry, question, love, and look at ourselves, the world and our fellow humans more perceptively.

Consider this a gallery exhibit in book form. Because much of the work is undated, I did not attempt a strict chronological organization. I have arranged the pieces to highlight each for its own merits as well as to place it in a technical and/or thematic context. Some of the texts have been transcribed for legibility and lightly edited. The title comes from the short poem on page 63. Remembrances of Van, family photos and biographical notes have been collected at the end of the book, along with acknowledgments for the many people who assisted with this effort.

My heartfelt thanks to Van's family and loved ones for their cooperation and trust. They gave me free rein to assemble this book as I thought best. Van's art was my sole inspiration. I have tried to act as an extension of him in organizing a whole that is as expressive and intriguing as its components.

—ZLG

The Collection

Linocut, 6.75"x 6.75"

Handwritten text on notebook paper.

Like spreading oil, dropping deeply into the infinite water only to be pushed back to lose itself on the surface. Never knowing the shadows of great depths.

Like a falling alabaster egg, a white rushing without direction, but steadily pulled down to crush upon the ice grey concrete, in fury and spite, within the second to relax and creep back towards the center, the broken yellow. Unable to regain the whole, to lose the will, to let go and remain destroyed and become covered in dust by the sticky wetness left by the struggle.

Like a clown with a futile audience, neither knowing what to do. Too absurd, too personal, too clearly close, too strained a distance. So both joke without laughter, or laugh on the edge of the nothing which waits for us all. Neon lights knowing the rites of the vacant night slowly, patiently, wait to eat those eyes which for too long a moment lose the saving distraction of nervous, mistlike noise, and so stare at the opening screams from beyond the door, beneath the floor. To squeeze the stillness from your ears to knock in your heart, to see yourself from beneath those solid eyes, and so to know the betrayal of trust, to have had an echo of reason as to why and like tea pot steam whistling its departure. Words shaping masses of moist fecund feeling into hard crystal thoughts which never are true. A total page of white covered by red, dark, dying blood rinsed with cold glass tears.

Serigraph, 9.5"x 7"

Serigraph, 7"x 7"

Linocut, 5.75"x 5.5"

Four pencil studies on paper, approx. 6”x 6”.
Clockwise from top left: ”Silver,” “7B&4H,” “7B&6H,” “Aluminum”

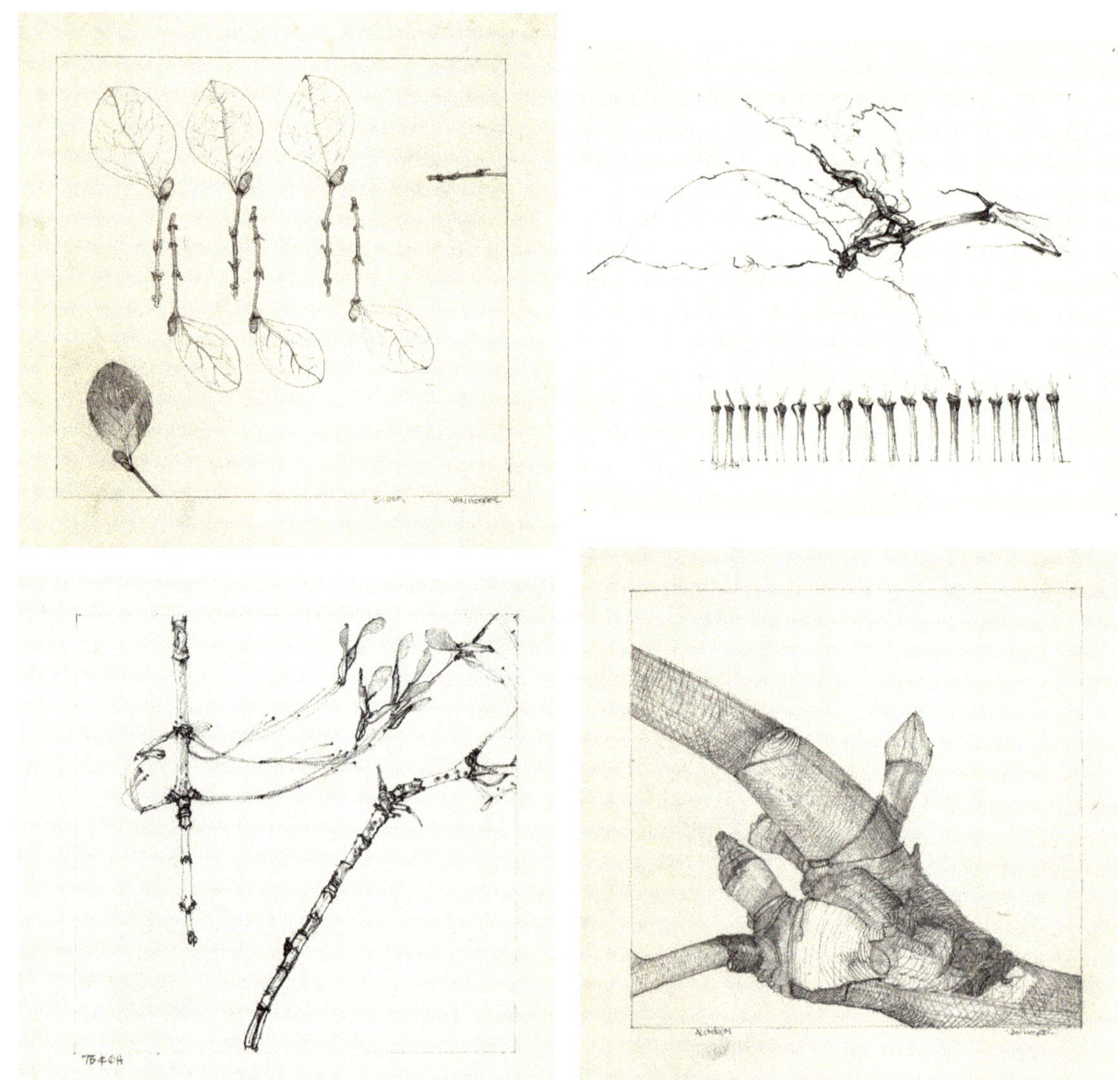

Ink on paper, 10.5”x 8.25”

Typed poems.

A blue sky absorbing time in its graceless fall
into the mists of passing nightclouds, white
beneath a distant,sun,not so different then as now
only a ~~vaccume~~ vacuum between the eye and the light
unseen as the grey sun curls away
into a swirling rush of hurrying night

On the edge of day, beyond death's rainbow
I run on the sands of our delight, with smiles
and empty ocean, drifting without moon or stars
gazing from darkness upon ~~a the~~ sparkling miles
of a world crystalizing with brightness delicate
for a moment's beauty passing into grey files
of imagined memories ansd merciful angels

BLACK SAHARA

Without the mercy of imagened angels
a bright sun would each day shine upon me
& a blue sky absorbing time in its graceless fall
into the mists of passing nightclouds
alien to a sparkling earth in darkness

Ink on notebook paper.

Poem “Your Nameless Face” handwritten on notebook paper; and two ink drawings approx. 9-1/2”x 7”.

YOUR NAMELESS FACE

I SEE THE SURFACE OF YOUR LIFE
AS YOU PASS ACROSS MINE
AS THROUGH GLASS I SEE
A DEPTH BEYOND MY FINGERS
YOU ARE IMPOSSIBLE TO REACH

TWO BODIES IN THE VOID
FROM BENEATH MY IMAGE
I GAZE INTO THE DREAM
I'VE MADE OF YOU

I DO NOT EXIST, YOU CANNOT SEE ME
& SO I AM ALONE IN TIME

ALONE IN TIME / YOUR NAMELESS FACE

I SEE THE SURFACE OF YOUR LIFE
AS YOU FLOW PAST MINE

I'M ALONE IN TIME
FLOATING IN MY SILENCE
UNABLE BY CIRCUMSTANCE
DISABLED BY COINCIDENCE

I GAZE AT THE IMAGE I'VE
MADE OF YOU, A DREAM
WITHOUT SENSE

Linocut on paper, 6”x 7”

Watercolor, 4.75"x 9.25"

Serigraph, 12”x 18”

Doodles on notebook paper.

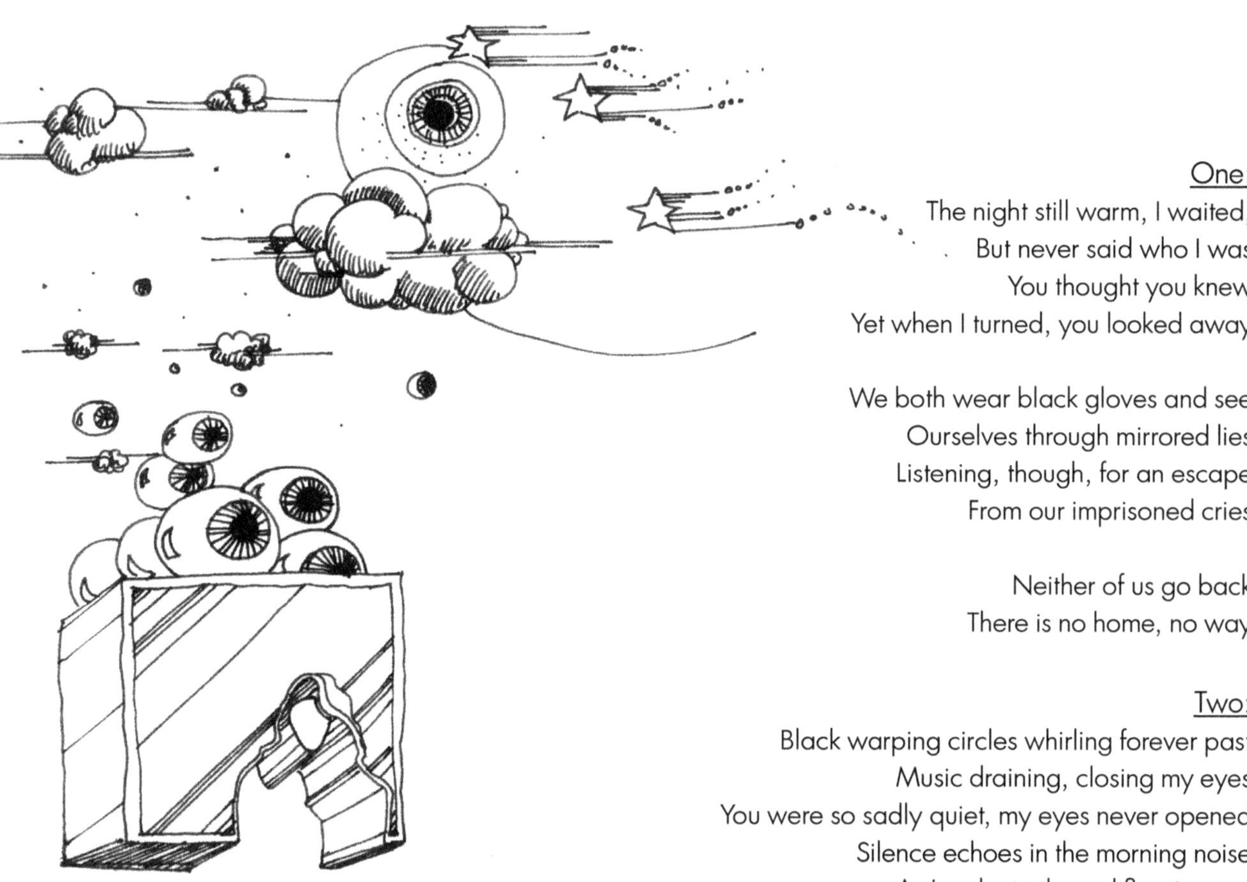

<u>One:</u>

The night still warm, I waited,
But never said who I was
You thought you knew
Yet when I turned, you looked away

We both wear black gloves and see
Ourselves through mirrored lies
Listening, though, for an escape
From our imprisoned cries

Neither of us go back
There is no home, no way

<u>Two:</u>

Black warping circles whirling forever past
Music draining, closing my eyes
You were so sadly quiet, my eyes never opened
Silence echoes in the morning noise
As I wake to the red floating sun
Rising stiffly in stifling stuffed empty air

I'm here usually, but not often
Do not come by unless you hear
Me filling the vacant rustling of breathing
Despair

Class assignment, handwritten on notebook paper.

Van Hooker
English 50
Oct. 4th 1973

ONE:

The nights still warm, I waited,
but never said who I was
You thought you knew
Yet when I turned, you looked away

We both wear black gloves and see
Ourselves through mirrored lies
Listening, though, for an escape
from our imprisoned cries.

Neither of us go back
There is no home, no way

TWO: Black warping circles whirling forever past
Music draining, closing my eyes
You were so sadly quiet, my eyes never opened
Silence echos in the morning noise
as I wake to the red floating sun
rising stiffly in stifling stuffed empty air

I'm here usually, but ~~often~~ not often
Do not come by unless you hear
me filling the vacant rustling of breathing
despair

Notebook cover, 6"x 9.5." Entries are from October 1973 through February 1974.

The dissolving man, looked
Too much on his self
Until there was no more to
Discover. Yet he looked more
Deeply into his image
And began to fade
Soon he became less of
What he was & more of no-
Thing he knew
The void crept in one night to
Steal him away to beyond
He is less and less
And no more but he is
Still here
Now he sees himself
Now, no
Gone and going he knows
That he is no more

Blue Notebook, pages 1-6, with selected transcriptions.

Alone the starblossom sleeps
Above a rush of falling lives
Silently running still
To the sea

Beside in invisible currents
Whirls the wet and
Aching hollow heads of
Unloved friends

Barren and bare
The universe only stare
Looking without eyes
To the seas

Unchanged
And unfilled

The fragile emptiness
Breaks in self illusion
Of death

Tears on icy walls freeze
Dry cold lips crack open
To cry unheard
Finger numb tips feel
The absence

Plucked
Black trees bare
And fruitless die
In blinding barreness
The souls rise from
The melted tombs
To harden under the
Eyeless dark of her moon

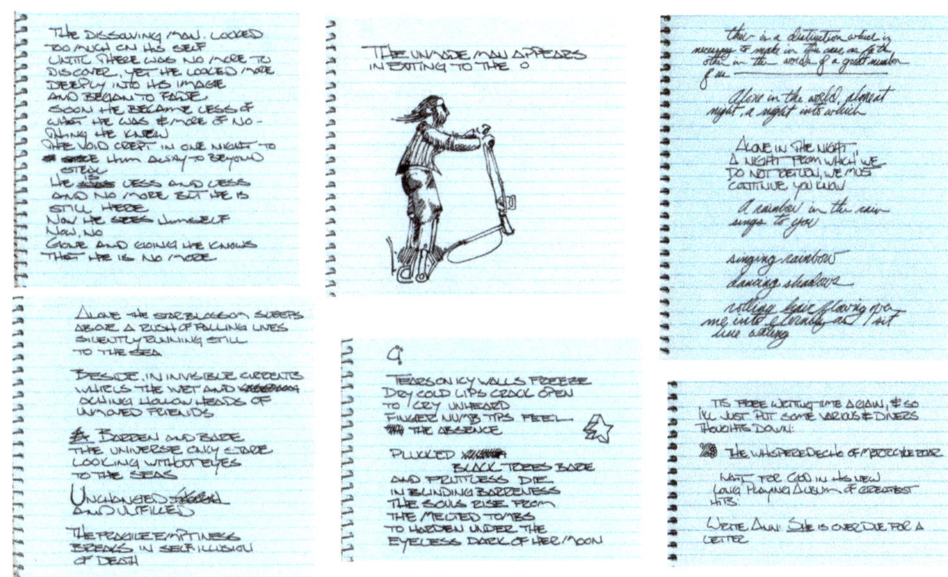

Blue Notebook, pages 7-11 with selected transcriptions.

Body & Time

Conspirators to make me old
& wise & immortal

I want to die in the summer
Too cold in the winter

Won't I ever get warm,
Cold so long
My head is getting numb
Touch me, hold me
Before I freeze or I won't
Know I'm gone

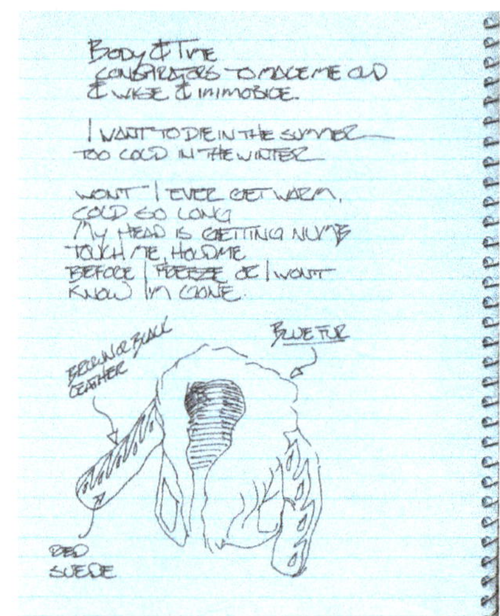

Chorus

My life is like a grave
My life is like a grave

Alone, so alone in my tomb
Will I ever see light again
Nothing I do makes any sense
& The darkness waits by the door

I try to wake up, but there is no day
My dreams do not end
Movement without form
Been getting worse since I was born.

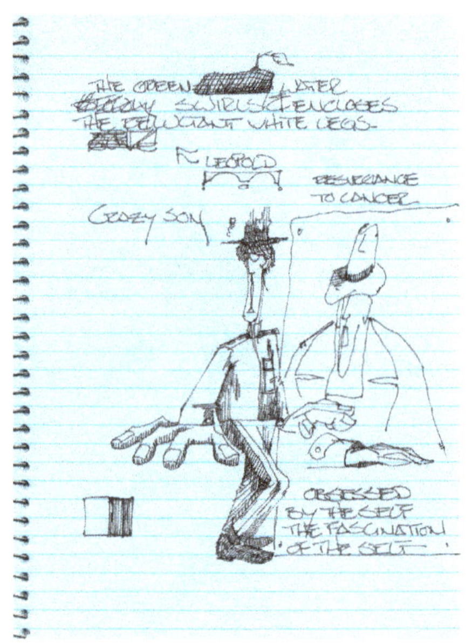

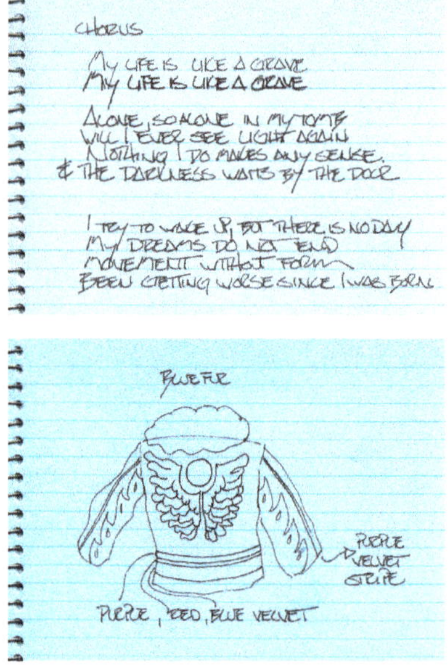

Marker on matboard, 7"x 7"

Ink drawings: Charger, 5"x 8.5"(published in the 1972 Albuquerque Academy Yearbook); Singer 2"x 4.5"

CHARGER 1972

Albuquerque
Academy

Ink on paper, 7"x 6"cartoon published in the 1972 Albuquerque Academy Yearbook; signed: El Nihilo 5/26/72.

Text, handwritten on notebook paper.

As western society moves further and further from the organized structure of Christianity as a means of explaining the universe, the responsibility becomes more and more the individual's to create some order or structure which deals with the themes of life. In effect each person must create a new cosmos filled with gods and heroes of his own making. The strain of this can be seen in today's fragmentation of Western culture. There are really no unifying structures unless it is the heart of destruction from the outside. The dehumanization of our civilization has been going on for many centuries, separating ourselves from nature, and, more importantly, from ourselves. This lack of contact with the environment and from each other results in increasing desperate attempts to reconcile the distance.

The past two hundred years have contained some of the most violent gestures of humanity. Destruction of many sanctioned orders, governments, ideas, it is not surprising then that the form of art should reflect the conflict within the civilization. More and more the application of scientific knowledge has created increasingly less organic machines. It would seem that as a result of the objectification which is being presented, man is seeking his organic connection back to the earth and to his own self.

The artist then becomes less a decorator of surfaces and a medium through which reality is achieved than he is a member of our present society who is able to bring together those incomprehensible forces which are in all of us and our existence. Perhaps because of the intensity of his vision the artist feels compelled to share it. To be an artist an audience is a prerequisite.

The artist is becoming then an important link with a part of ourselves which has been slowly left to die as we cultivate a control over and a distance from each other.

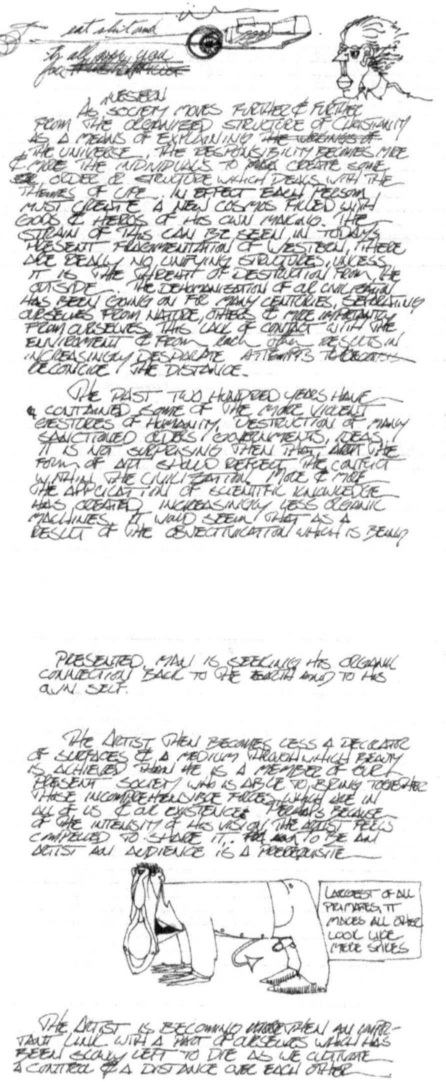

Illustrated class notes, ink on notebook paper.

Illustrated class notes and cartoons.

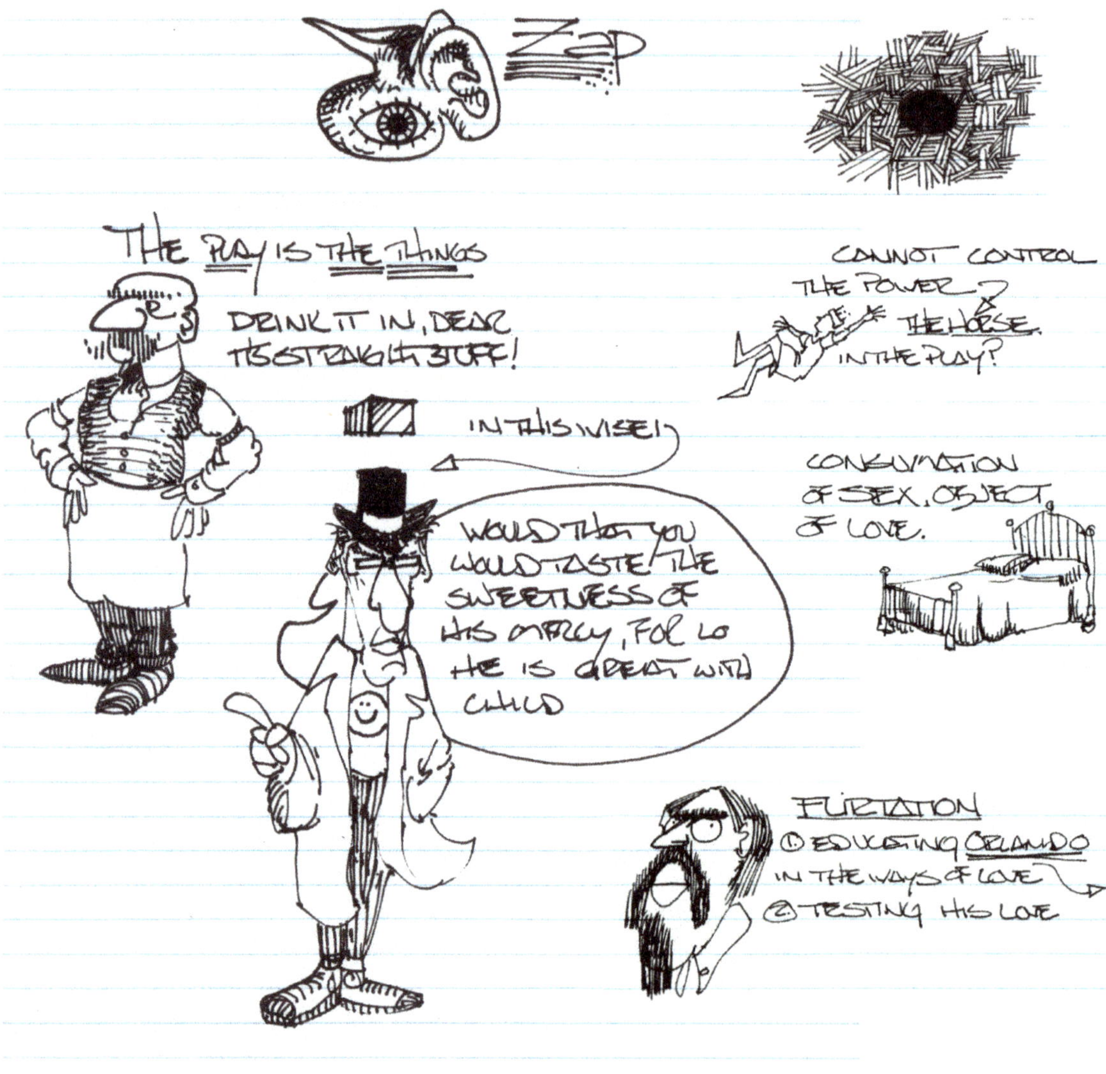

Illustrated class notes, 1974.
Illustrated class notes, undated.

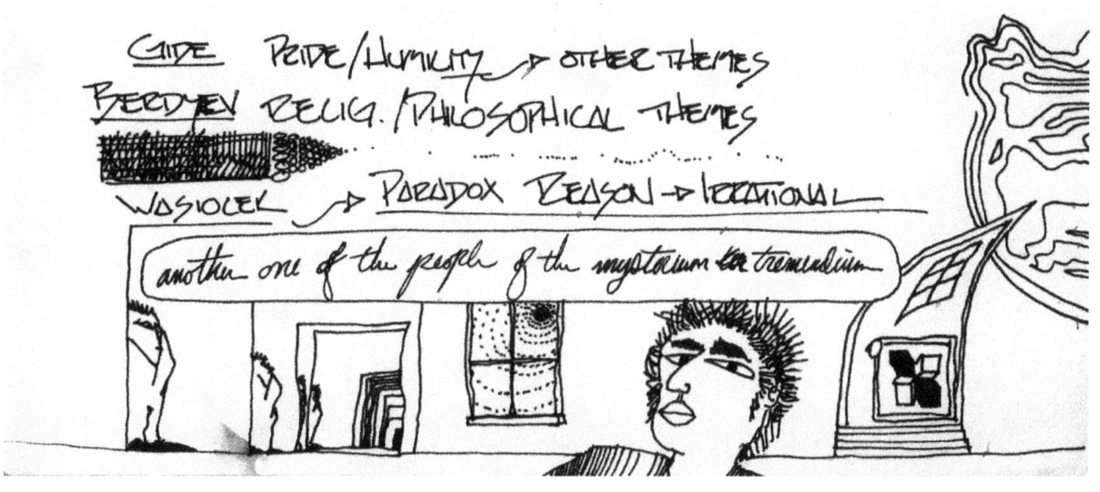

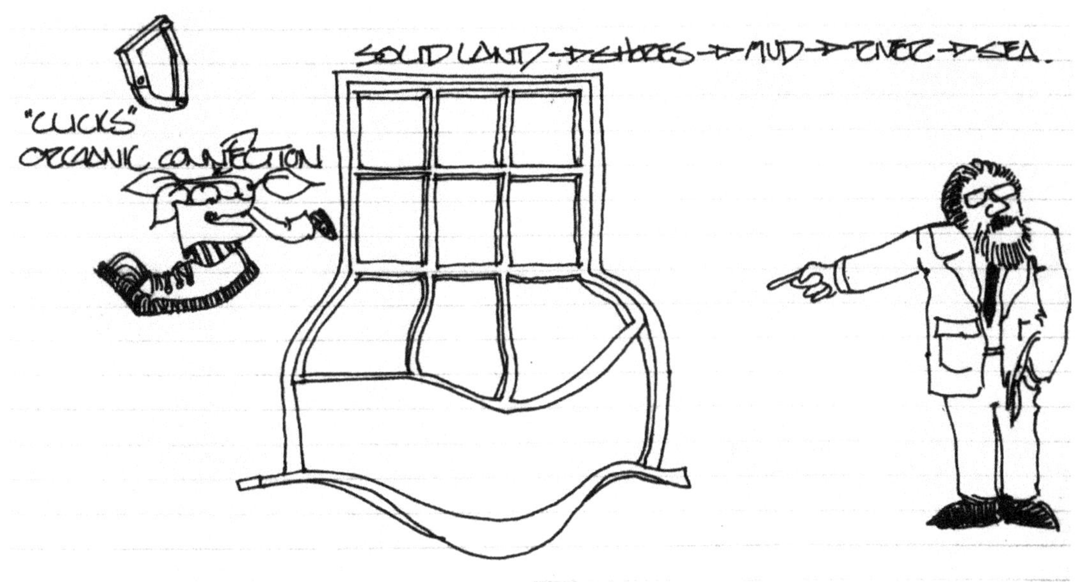

Sketches and cartoons.

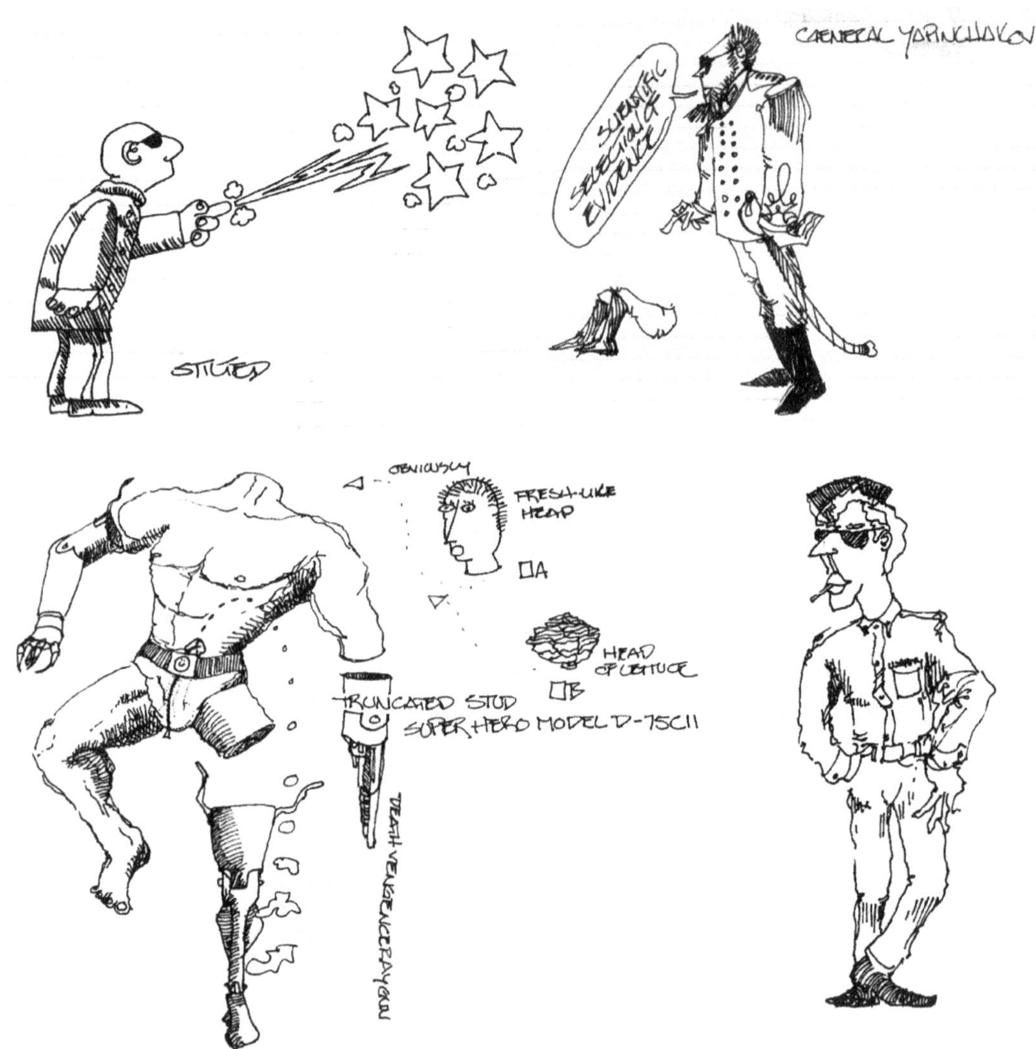

Ink on paper, 6"x 4," "The Magician," signed: El Nihilo 5/26/72.

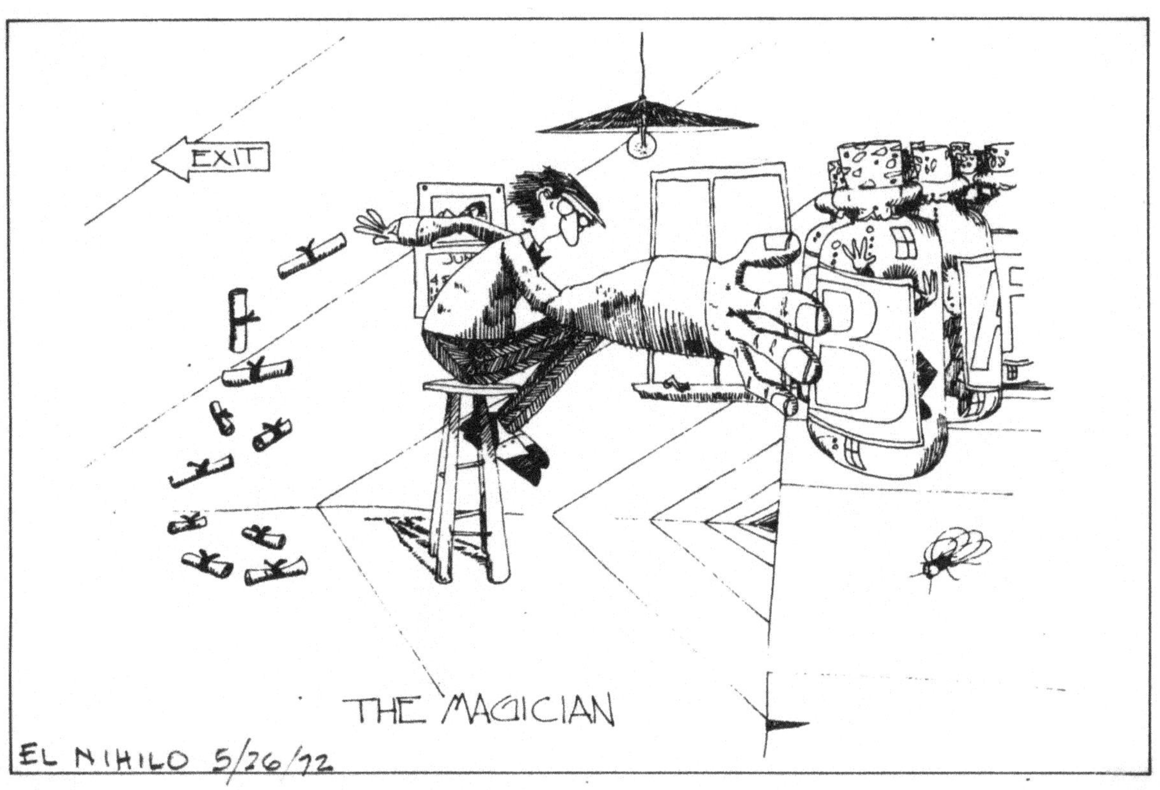

Cartoons and notes on back of typed pages.

Ink on notebook paper.

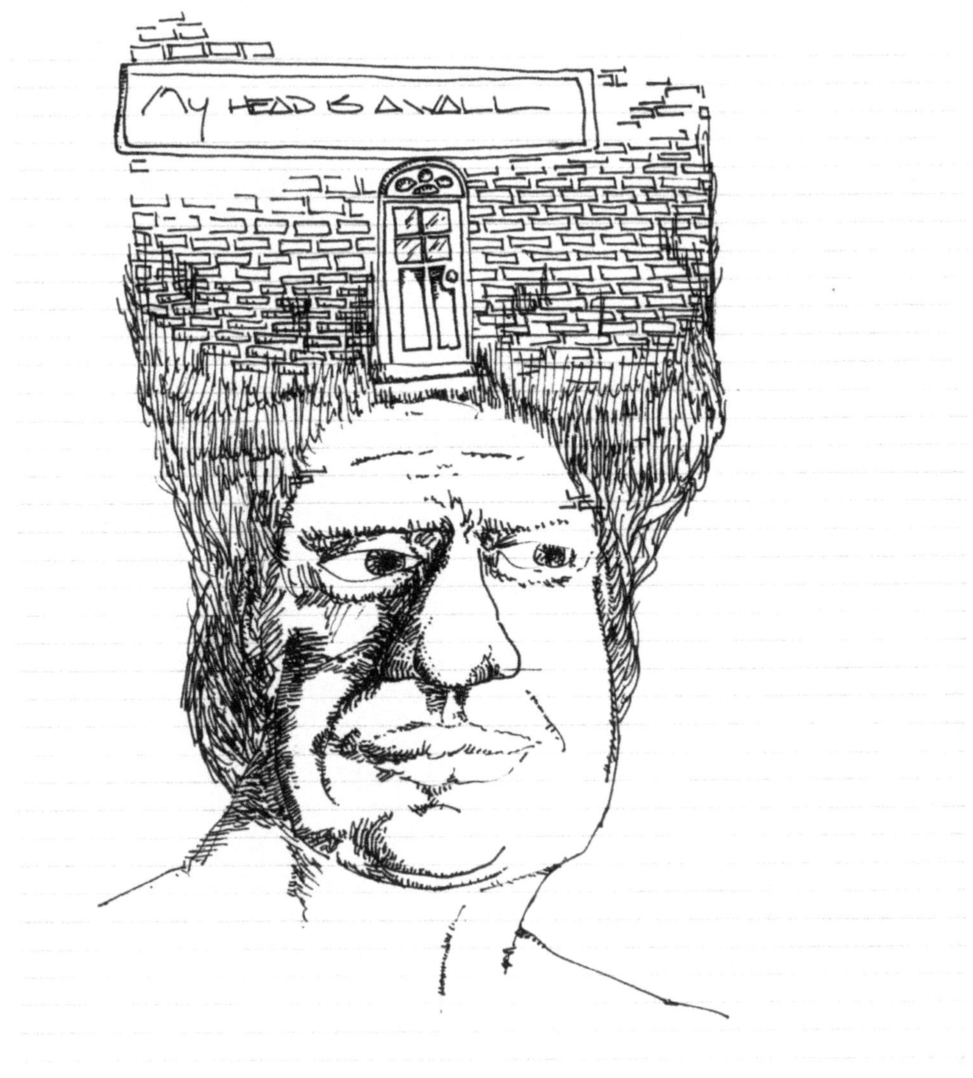

Ink on notebook paper.

Illustrated class notes and cartoons; excerpt from letter to Kurt.

Ink on notebook paper.

A CONFUSION OF THE SENSES MAKES FOR A CONFUSION.

I'M IGNORANT

PROFESSED CHRISTIANS THERE IS AN ABSOLUTE TRUTH. THERE IS TRUTH.

THAT'S A REMARKABLE STATEMENT

BELIEVE IN GOD, JESUS

RUNNING OUT OF TIME

Ink on notebook paper.

VOICES SOUND UPON THE DEEP TOO FAR TO REACH, TOO NEAR TO FORGET, CLOSE BUT UNTOUCHED, IRON FENCES ARE FINE DEFENCES TO MIND THE APPROACH OF FEAR.

ZAPPA YEATS!

SHE GROWS A BARREN DISTANCE
A FERTILE ROAD
IT'S ALL RIGHT, IT SEEMS
SHE CAN FIND HER HEART
ON HER RECORD PLAYER
AND LOOK FOR MR. GOODNIGHT
TO RIDE FROM THE MOCKFUL STARS
SO SERIOUS, SO FURIOUS
SO INTERIOR, SO SUPERIOR

DYLAN CIRCLES YOUR SOUL, & YOU THINK YOU KNOW WHAT HE SAID, SAD-EYED PERSON

MAKING FUN, BEING SERIOUS WORDS FILL YOU UP &

SARCASM
CYNICISM
RIDICULE
TRUTH
HONESTY
TRUST

NO RELIEF FROM WORDS
PRETTY, UGLY, UNSEEN,
KNOWN.
LAUGHTER/MUST RELIEVE
GREATER & GREATER TENSIONS
HOW AWARE OR HOW DEAD
MUSH, MUSH

WHY ART. NO ANSWERS
WRONG QUESTIONS, BUT
WHY CAN YOU ASK QUESTIONS
FOR WHICH THERE AREN'T ANY
ANSWERS? HOW COME, HUH?

Ink on notebook paper.

Notecard to Kurt.

Notes and cartoons from school papers, journal and letter to Holly.

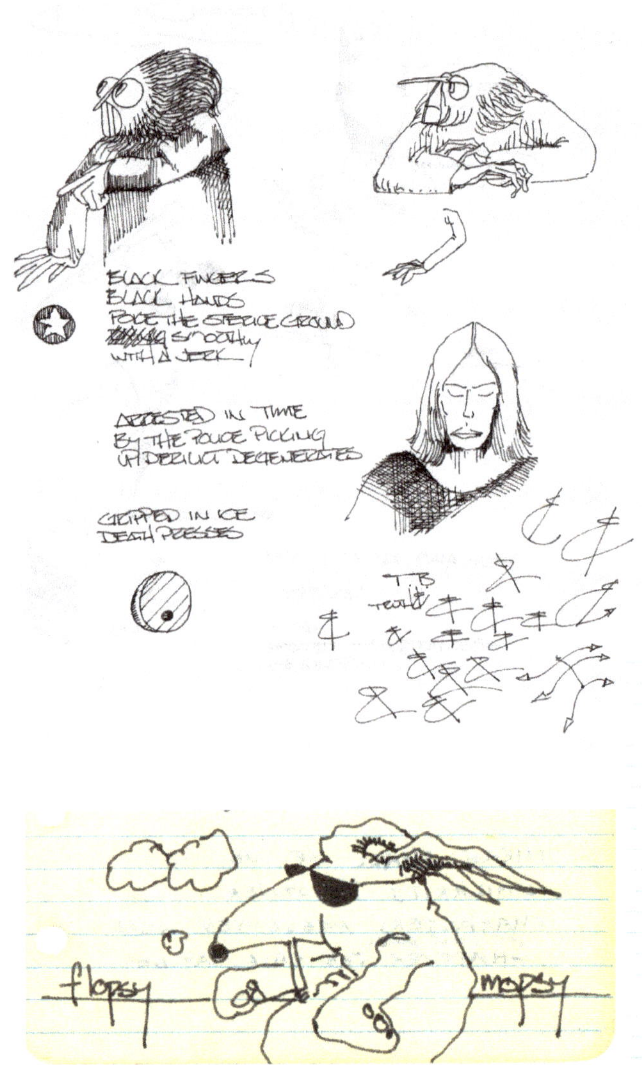

Marker on cardboard.

Composition book: cover, cover detail and first page.

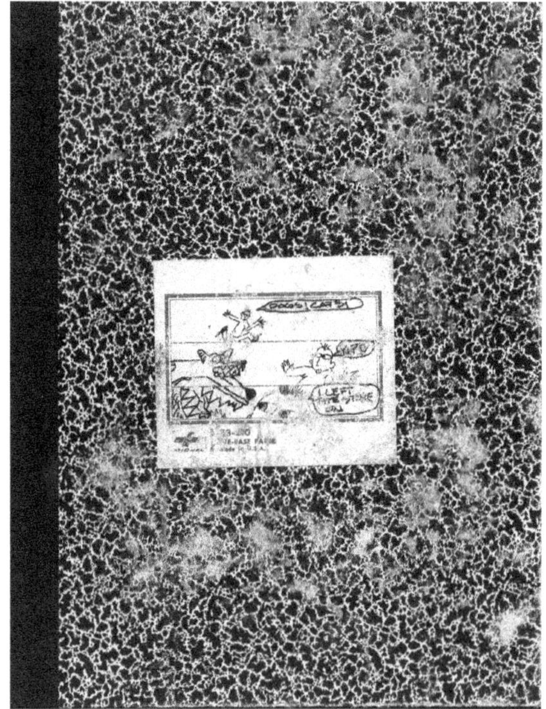

I STEPPED FROM THE HILL AND FLEW
THE BODY OF THE WORLD SLIPPED BENEATH ME
AS I PASSED ON WHISPERING LEAVES
BRANCHES AND HILLS ROLLED AND FLED
ON A BREEZE

THE HEAVEN'S CLOUDS LIKE DREAMS
THE SKY LIKE SLEEP, THE SUN THE EYES
OF DEAD DOGS WHO DIED BY RIVERS
THE BIRDS FLIES ON THE THE FLESH OF
THOSE PALE PHANTOMS

I STEPPED FROM THE HILL AND FELL
ALL VANISHING AS I SLIPPED OVER THE DIRT
INTO NIGHT'S PAIN

I stepped from the hill and flew
The body of the world slipped beneath me
As I passed on whispering leaves
Branches and hills rolled and fled
On a breeze

The heaven's clouds like dreams
The sky like sleep, the sun the eyes
Of dead dogs who died by rivers
The birds flies on the flesh of
Those pale phantoms

I stepped from the hill and fell
All vanishing as I slipped over the dirt
Into night's pain

School assignment.
Drawing from letter to Holly.

An ant sat on the table cloth
As I ate my bats head broth
In reverence of the drying blood
Yet moist within my head does flood
My life with picnic squares of black
And red, and hard eggs that hatch
Brooding solemn, monkish chicks
And dry watermelon's thick
Rinds waiting to confound me

That impish ant did see said he
I was eating my left foot
In sunlight lit with dusty soot
Laughing, laughing, most carefully
The happy silly little beast
Tore my fool's heart from off my knee
And ate his part of my feast

Drink all your lemonade hear
But cry not that reflecting tear
That blinds your dismal eye
To implicit sorrow and the fly

Van Hooker
Creative Writing
Oct. 9th, 1973

An ant sat on the table cloth
As I ate my bats head broth
In reverence of the drying blood
Yet moist within my head does flood
My life with picnic squares of black
And red, and hard eggs that hatch
Brooding solemn, monkish chicks
And dry watermelon's thick
Rinds waiting to confound me

That impish ant did see said he
I was eating my left foot
In sunlight lit with dusty soot
Laughing, laughing, most carefully
The happy silly little beast
Tore my fool's heart from off my knee
And ate his part of my feast

Drink all your lemonade hear
But cry not that reflecting tear
That blinds your dismal eye
To implicit sorrow and the fly

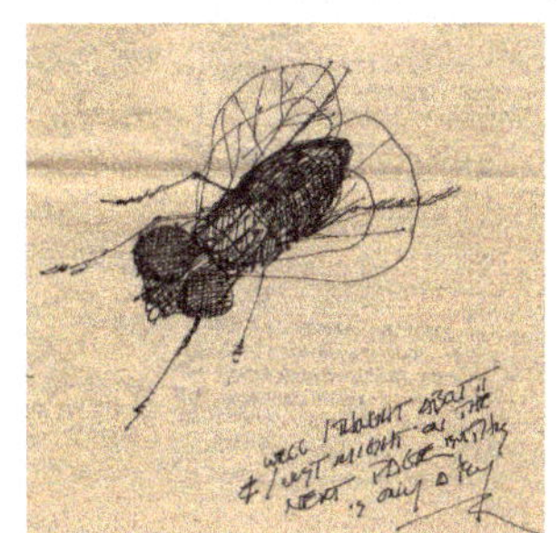

Ink on notebook paper.

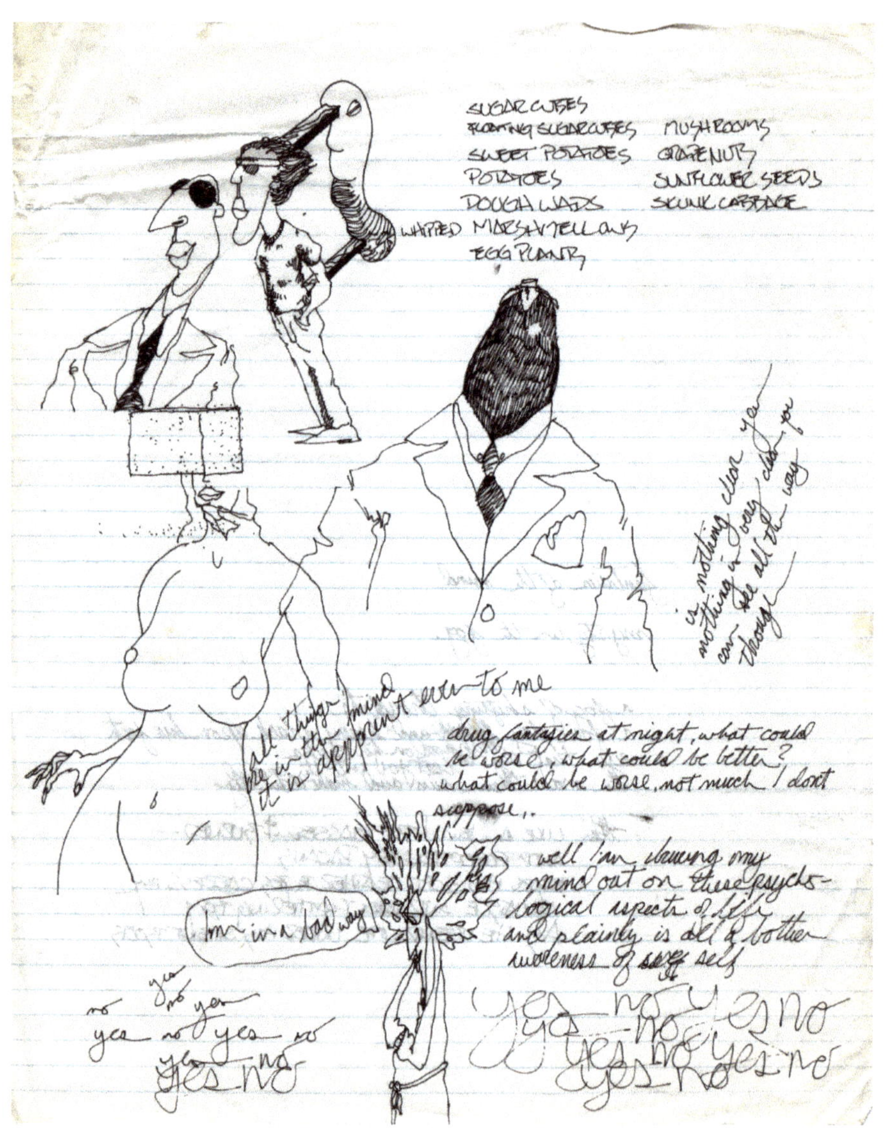

Ink drawing - reproduction, 9"x 12"

“Islands in the Dream” typed poems.

islands in the dream, i woke in the vacant stream
the time touched me in the night, and i woke
into the lightless day, burned black by the clotted sun
suspended in jelly of space
yes yes yes i cried and i saw the drunk
crash into the emptiness on the infinity of grey
which keeps the black asphalt rivers from leaping
into the mind
sidewalks on the rivers of death
flowing and swirling around the
empty crypts side by each other
eack day relieved of their burden
and then to wearily receive them
once the sun collapses again into
the flawed horizon

over and over into the water
over and over we drown
the swirling green crystalizing
our lives into passing foam

```
islands in the dream, i woke in the vacant stream
the time touchedme in the night, and i woke
into the lightless day, burned black by the clotted sun
suspended in the  jelly of space
yes yes yes i cried and i saw the drunk
crash into the emptiness on the infinity of grey
which keeps the black asphalt rivers from leaping
into the mind
sidewalks on the rivers of death
flowing and swirling around the
empty crypts side by each other
eack day releived of their burden
and then to wearily reciee them
once the sun collapses again into
the flawed horison


over and over into the water
over and over we drown
the swirling green crystalizing
our lives into passing foam

bears and the n

bear attack at night

we sat and listened but
the night only breathed at us ho ho hoho

again and again we sought the a
the souce sssississiskdkdkd ddkdkdkkkkdkdkdk kdkkdkdkdkdkdkdkdkdkekkdk

oodkkdeokdkkfjvnm8u888e888e8e8eii8e888e88e8e88e88e88e847564756475 87466


½ of all our domestic and foreign relations have by this time
become of little or no further value to our policy of expanding
 awareness here and abroad, however it will be possibe to
```

Ink on paper, 7.25"x 7"

Ink on paper, 6"x 6.5"

B/W Photo, 9"x 7"

Piece of plywood inked and printed, 12”x 16”

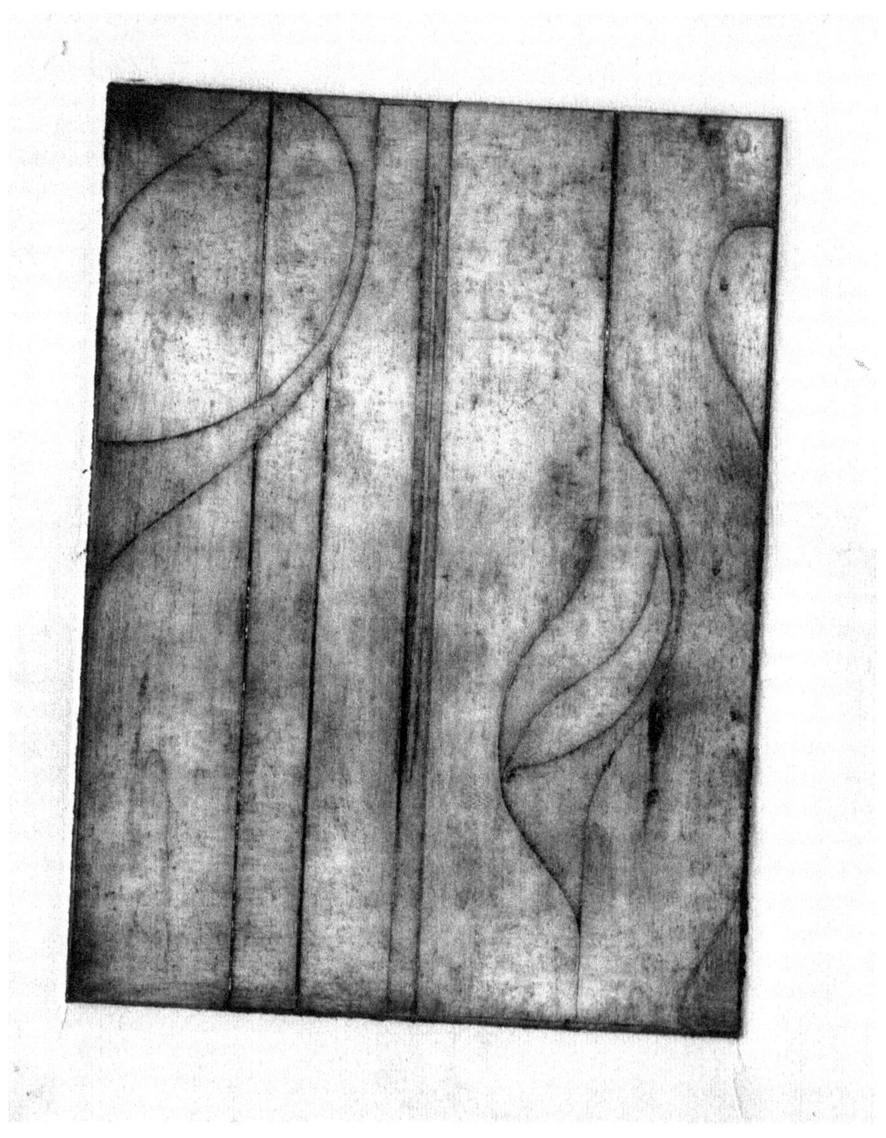

B/W photos, 7"x 9"

B/W photo, 4"x 6"

B/W Photo, 6"x 4"

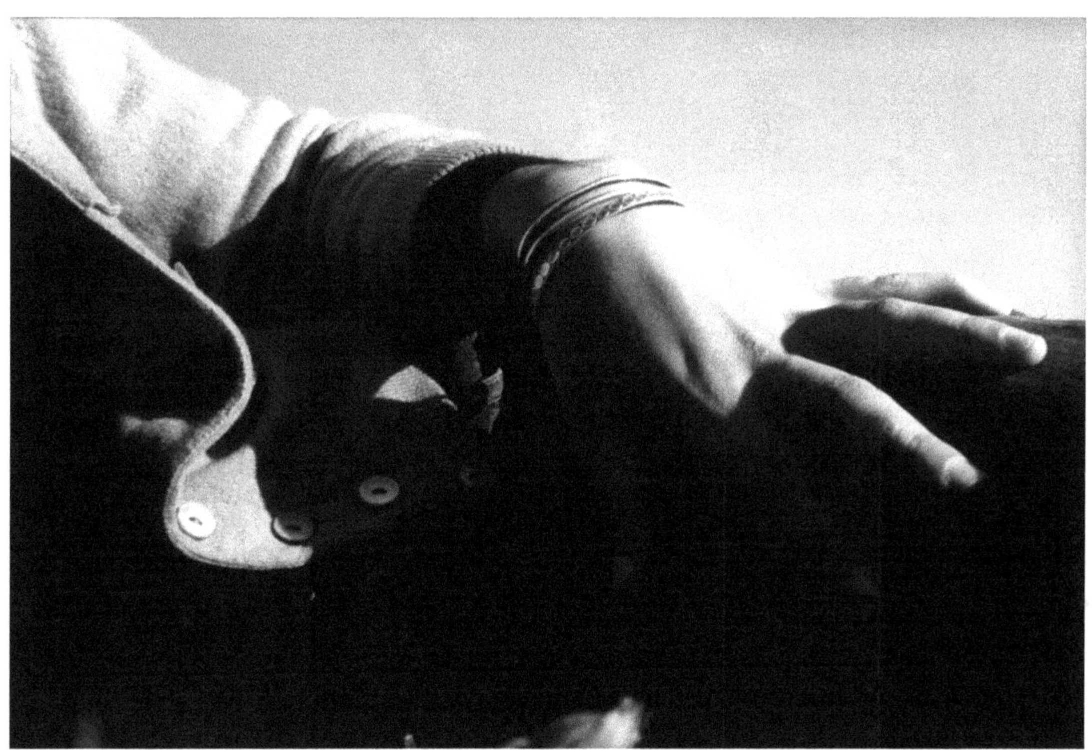

B/W Photo, 7”x 9”

B/W Photo, 6.5"x 4.5" and short poem on notebook paper.

THE WIND WAITS FOR ME
TO BLOW ME TO THE SUNSET
IT COMES BY EVERY DAY
TO BRING ME TO THE EDGE OF MY LIFE
BUT I SIT & WAIT TOO
TO BE READY TO GO

B/W Photo, 6.5"x 4.5"

Dada Series #3 Desire, collage on board, 11.75"x 11.75": This series of collages on board, heavyweight paper and tracing paper was apparently designed to be layered and sequenced in a variety of ways. A selection of the work is presented here in one possible arrangement. ed.

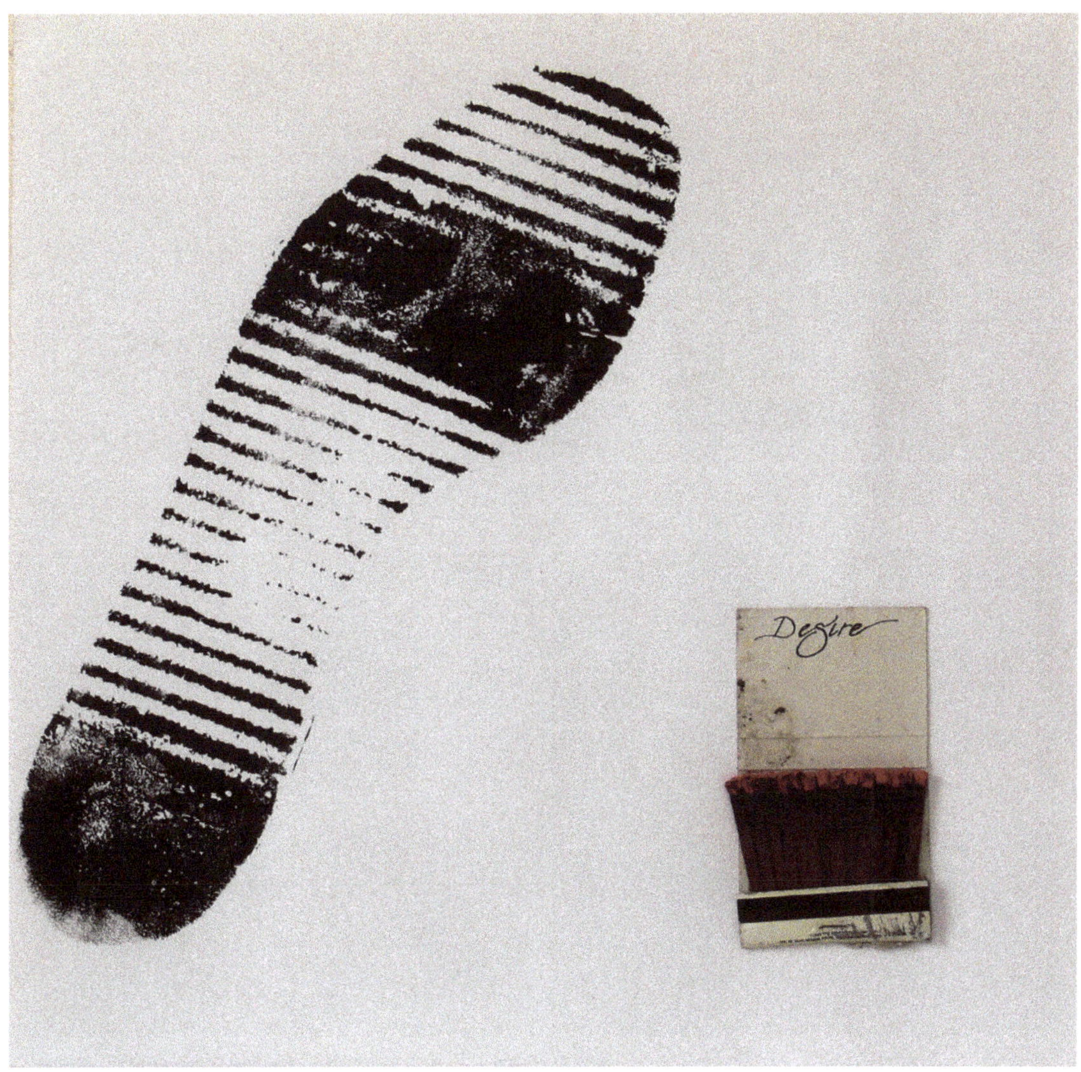

Dada Series; clockwise from top left: #1 Winstead's, collage on board; #2 V Rex, calligraphy, ink on board; #3+#4 digital double exposure by ed.; #3 Map, paper on board.

Dada Series; clockwise from top left: #6 Footprint, ink on tracing paper; #6 with #7 Fonts, paper collage/cut-out; #8 "C" collage on board; #5 Forgotten Years, collage on board.

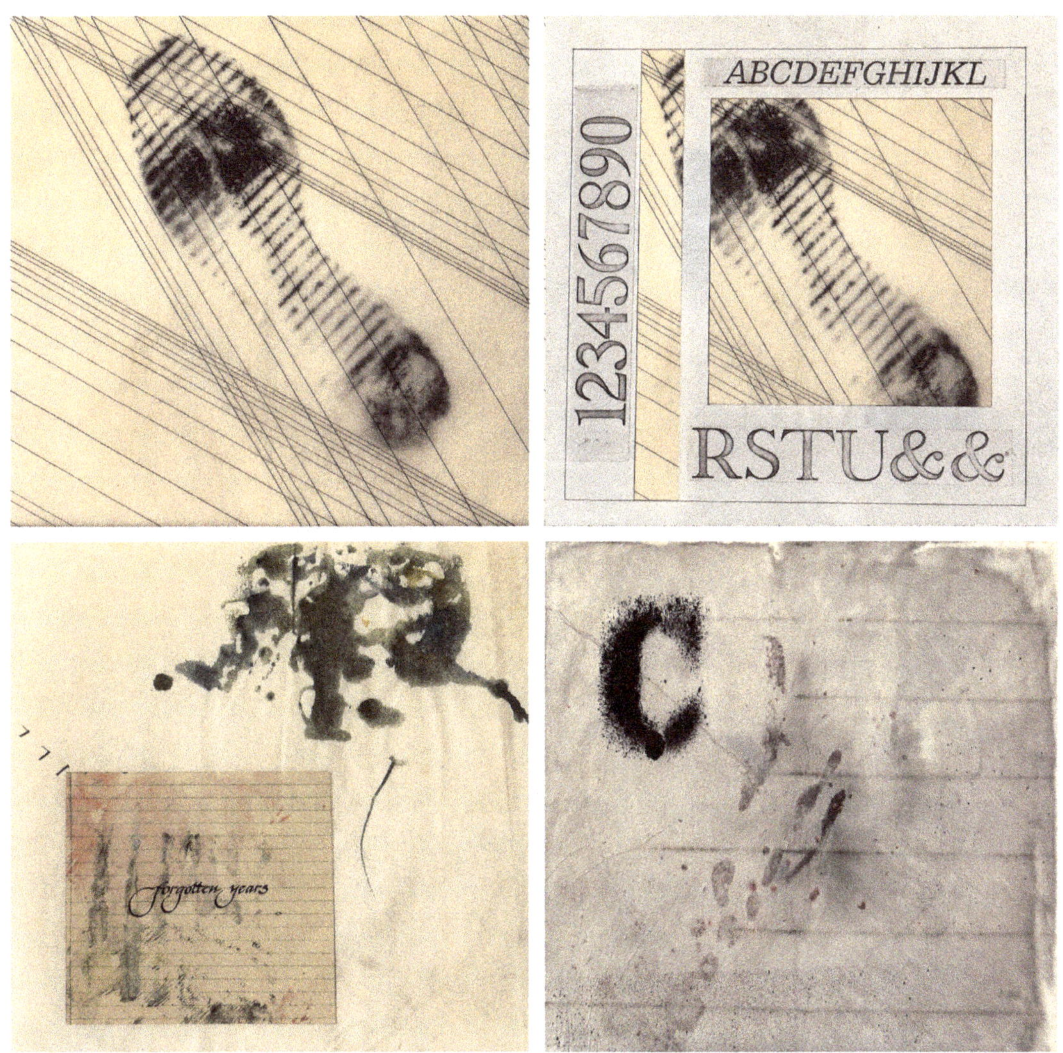

"I Am In Dreams" from letter to Holly; and 7"x 4.75" B/W photo, taken in Kansas City.

A LOVE POEM
(WHEN EVERYONE IS A TUBE)
FROM THE LDB —

I AM IN DREAMS

WITHOUT THE MERCY OF IMAGINED ANGELS:
A FUTILE LIFE AND EMPTY DEATH
UNDER THE CLOTTED SUN
WHERE LIFE ENDS BEFORE IT BEGINS
AND NO ONE EVER LEFT, NO ONE
EVER RAN

A ROTTING WING AND CADILLAC LIES
OF THE SHORT AND FAT
AND PROPER WAYS TO KILLING DREAMS
RIDE WITH ME AT NIGHT
ACROSS MY ASPHALT WONDERLAND

A BLUE SKY ABSORBING TIME IN ITS GRACELESS FALL
FROM THE SUN I SEE THE WIND
DRIFTING WITHOUT A MOON OR STARS

CAUGHT ON THE EDGE OF DAY, BEYOND DEATH'S RAINBOW
I RUN ON THE SANDS OF OUR DELIGHT
CASTING FROM SUMMER'S SHADOW
UPON A SPARKLING DREAM
OF A WORLD CRYSTALIZING FOR A MOMENT'S BEAUTY PASSING
INTO THE DISTANCE, NOT SO DIFFERENT THEN AS NOW,
OF THE VACANCY BETWEEN THE EYE AND THE LIGHT.
UNSEEN AS THE GREY CURLS AWAY
INTO THE SWIRLING RUSH OF ANGRY NIGHT

A THOUSAND DREAMS DIED LEAVING LIKE FORGOTTEN TRAINS
NOW EVERYONE RIDES THE BLACKTOP EXPRESS
HANDS OF ICE, EYES SO NICE.
A MACHINE ATE MY MOTHER
I HAVE THE BONES IT LEFT, POISONING MY BRAINS.

FROM A ROOM OF DIRTY WALLS OF WASTED YEARS
AND THE TORMENTS OF MY MIND
YOUR ARMS AND YOUR BREATH
HELD MY LAUGHING SOUL.
MY HEART SMILES WITH YOUR LIPS
AND I CRY WITH USELESS EYES.
TOUCH ME AT NIGHT IN MY FLEEING DREAMS
AS I TOUCH YOU
BEYOND THE BITTER RAINS OF THE CANCER MEN
RUN WITH ME BY THE OCEAN
ON THE SANDS OF OUR DELIGHT

B/W photo, 7"x 4.75", taken in Kansas City.

Caught on the edge of day, beyond death's rainbow
I run on the sands of our delight
Gazing from summer's shadow
Upon a sparkling dream
Of a world crystallizing for a moment's beauty passing
Into the distance, not so different then as now,
Of the vacancy between the eye and the light,
Unseen as the grey curls away
Into the swirling rush of angry night

I Am In Dreams

Without the memory of imagined angels:
A futile life and empty death
Under the clotted sun
Where life ends before it begins
And no one ever left, no one
Ever ran

A rotting wind and Cadillac lies
Of the short and fat
And proper ways of killing dreams
Ride with me at night
Across my asphalt wonderland

A blue sky absorbing time in its graceless fall
From the sun I see the wind
Drifting without a moon or stars

A thousand dreams died, leaving like forgotten trains
Now everyone rides the black top express
Hands of ice, eyes so nice,
A machine ate my mother
I have the bones it left, poisoning my brains—

From a room of dirty walls of wasted years
And the torments of my mind
Your arms and your breath
Held my laughing soul.
My heart smiles with your lips
And I cry with useless eyes.
Touch me at night in my fleeing dreams
As I touch you
Beyond the bitter rains of the cancer men
Run with me by the ocean
On the sands of our delight

Crayon and pencil drawings in 11"x 14" pad.

B/W photos, 3.5"x 5.3", taken in Kansas City; and pencil on paper, from 12"x 18" pad.

Poem "Love's Winter" handwritten on notebook paper.

Love's Winter

Leaves in oil, in the asphalt's watery black -
A sidewalks cracks and weeds,
And a colder wind catches the fleeing
Exhaust, the departing red a little harder
Than before, lost into ripples of mind,
I think yet do not see the shadow
Cast. Nothing remains
In the fog's dissolving breath.

I might say lost, but more confused—
Smoke of the evening's gray dullness
Stands against the air
Nothing moves, I die
Nothing sounds. The world drops away
Beyond the graying edge

I am surrounded by darkening fog
A day's time vanishes into night
The evening's rest becomes morning's light
Without dreams.
Days of running time, burning
Life without edges, a mind forgets.

Please respond (your son is dying)
"He's already dead"
Something less than vegetable
More stone or ice or lead

A fraying whiteness comes to my lips
As I smile. Seeking a dreamer's joy
I fear my death is come

Peeled paint and cracked vinyl
Rusted doors and missing teeth
Defective by use.
Absorbed through neglect,
Vanished -

(cont. p. 74)

B/W photo, 6.75"x 4.3", double exposure.

"Love's Winter" pg. 2 (reverse side).

Still as I am, there is still the urge
To fill the hole I am, to breath, to eat
A persuasion to see;
The body lives apart.

And the mind sneaks in unseen
Caught by a mirrored face.
Up by its roots
My bloody tears fill the need.

Lightning without thunder, the flicker of bats
Across electric shadows, the edge
Of a rising flame, the beginning of a fading
Smoke, silence of night highway -
The eye of the winter's moon, the blood of
The summer's lust, the blindness of a mask
The empty clothes on the floor, I am less.

Your hand reaches for me, you have only my shadow
I've your dream. I've lost you in time
Reach for me again, and again, and again
To step from darker places

I cry for warmth

I'm cold

Persephone is stolen, & hidden by distance
I watch the sun fade and wait.

B/W photo, 4.75"x 3"

Photo 4.5"x 7" with "Exit Light" transcription compiled by ed.

"Exit Light"

In the gloom he appeared
To sit and stare
With an inward groan

He sought the lonely doom
Away he stretched his arm
to touch the void

Alone the star blossom sleeps
Above a rush of falling lives
Silently running still
to the sea

Beside, in invisible currents
Whirls the wet
and aching hollow heads
of unmoved friends

Barren and bare
The universe only stares
looking without eyes
to the seas

The vacuum of the soul
sucks the quiet meaning
of the world

Soft abandoned grass
catching dryly
the dancing hair

Night clouds flying with the wind
Gently over the ragged earth
All soft and sharp

All sharp and soft
Scratching at the dark
An apparition of the moon
In a sliding sky

Red burning eyes
One for the morning
The other for night

"Exit Light" drafts.

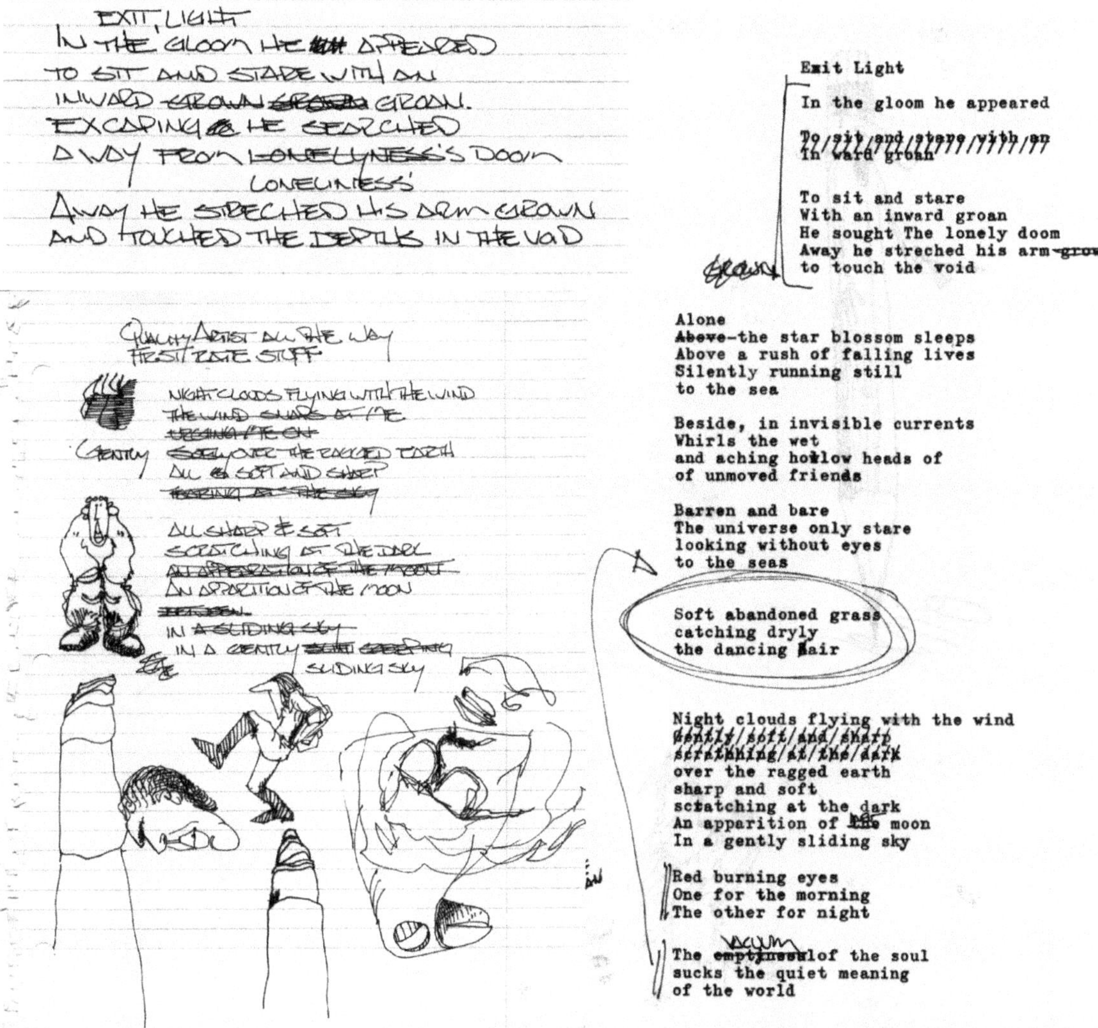

EXIT, LIGHT
IN THE GLOOM HE APPEARED
TO SIT AND STARE WITH AN
INWARD ~~GROWN~~ GROAN.
ESCAPING HE SEARCHED
A WAY FROM ~~LONELINESS'S~~ DOOM
LONELINESS'
AWAY HE STRECHED HIS ARM GROWN
AND TOUCHED THE DEPTHS IN THE VOID

QUALITY ARTIST ALL THE WAY
FIRST RATE STUFF

NIGHT CLOUDS FLYING WITH THE WIND
GENTLY ~~OVER THE RAGGED EARTH~~
ALL SHARP & SOFT
SCRATCHING AT THE DARK
AN APPARITION OF THE MOON
IN A GENTLY SLIDING SKY

Exit Light

In the gloom he appeared

~~To sit and stare with an~~
~~In ward groan~~

To sit and stare
With an inward groan
He sought The lonely doom
Away he streched his arm ~~grown~~
to touch the void

Alone
~~Above~~-the star blossom sleeps
Above a rush of falling lives
Silently running still
to the sea

Beside, in invisible currents
Whirls the wet
and aching hollow heads of
of unmoved friends

Barren and bare
The universe only stare
looking without eyes
to the seas

Soft abandoned grass
catching dryly
the dancing hair

Night clouds flying with the wind
~~Gently soft and sharp~~
~~scratching at the dark~~
over the ragged earth
sharp and soft
scratching at the dark
An apparition of ~~the~~ moon
In a gently sliding sky

Red burning eyes
One for the morning
The other for night

The ~~emptiness~~ vacuum of the soul
sucks the quiet meaning
of the world

B/W photo, 5.3”x 3.3” double exposure, and short text.

I AM IN DREAMS FLOWING GENTLY.
A BLUE SKY ABSORBING TIME
INTO THE MISTS OF PASSING CLOUDS
NOT SO DIFFERENT THEN AS NOW

B/W photo, 7”x 7.75”, and short text.

I DON'T LIKE THOSE EMPTY LOOKS
EMPTY EYES AND OPEN MOUTH
A GAPE AT ME.
SEEING NOTHING
I DON'T LIKE THOSE EMPTY LOOKS

PASS ME BY BUT DON'T LOOK
I MIGHT SEE THAT YOU DON'T CARE
THE DISTANCE BETWEEN YOU & ME
IS GREATER THAN WORDS OR AIR

B/W photo, 7.5"x 9.3", and short text.

LONELY MAN SEARCHING FOR HAPPINESS
SEES A THOUSAND FACES
BUT HE CANNOT REACH THOSE PEOPLE
IN THEIR ICY PLACES

Pencil drawings in 12"x 18" newsprint pad.

Pencil drawing in 12”x 18” sketch pad.

Pencil drawing in 12”x 18” newsprint pad.

Newsprint pad, 12"x 18", cover and detail.

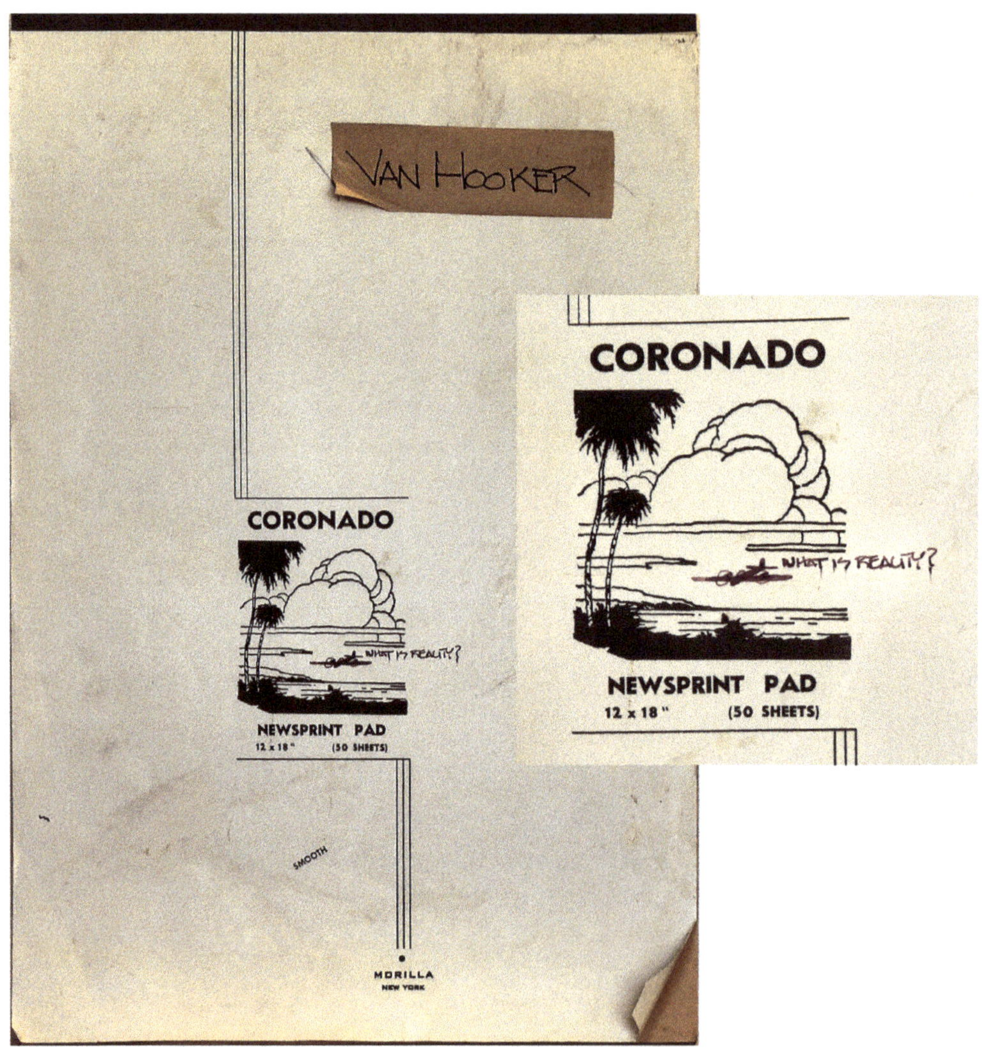

Letter, handwritten on notebook paper.

Jan 21st

Hey this is not funny. I got no money. But I guess that's my own fault. But do send something, mine yours anybody's as long as it will buy books & food. I'm going to starve soon & that will tear my grade-point average all up.

Dear Parents, (Father & Mother)

Ho! Now that you've heard again about my plight I'll tell you that my onions sprouted & so did my potatoes & turnips. And I've run out of eggs, cheese & milk. And I've overdrawn my account, for paint no less. Now I am really feeling the role of the poverty/artist struggling for materials. For his art. For a little while I've been tempted to go more & more for art & being a professional artist. Probably not the most secure fortune & I can begin to see those worry thoughts forming in your heads. Oh No, our grasshopper lay about son is going to be a for-sure bum, but with my good eye & general good taste, basic psychological torments and small gift of talent I might make good. But it's a pretty scary world to carry a vision around in.

Ink on paper: “Trying to Explain Disaster”

TRYING TO EXPLAIN DISASTER

BROKEN VIOLENCE ON DUSTY WINDOWS
TOO TIRED TO MOVE

THE WIND WILL COME BLOWING,
THE WIND WILL COME BLOWING
FROM AFAR

IT WILL SEE WHAT YOU'VE

THE WINTER IS
RISING

THE WINTER IS RISING
AS I TRY AND EXPLAIN

Lithograph, 12.5"x 8.5"

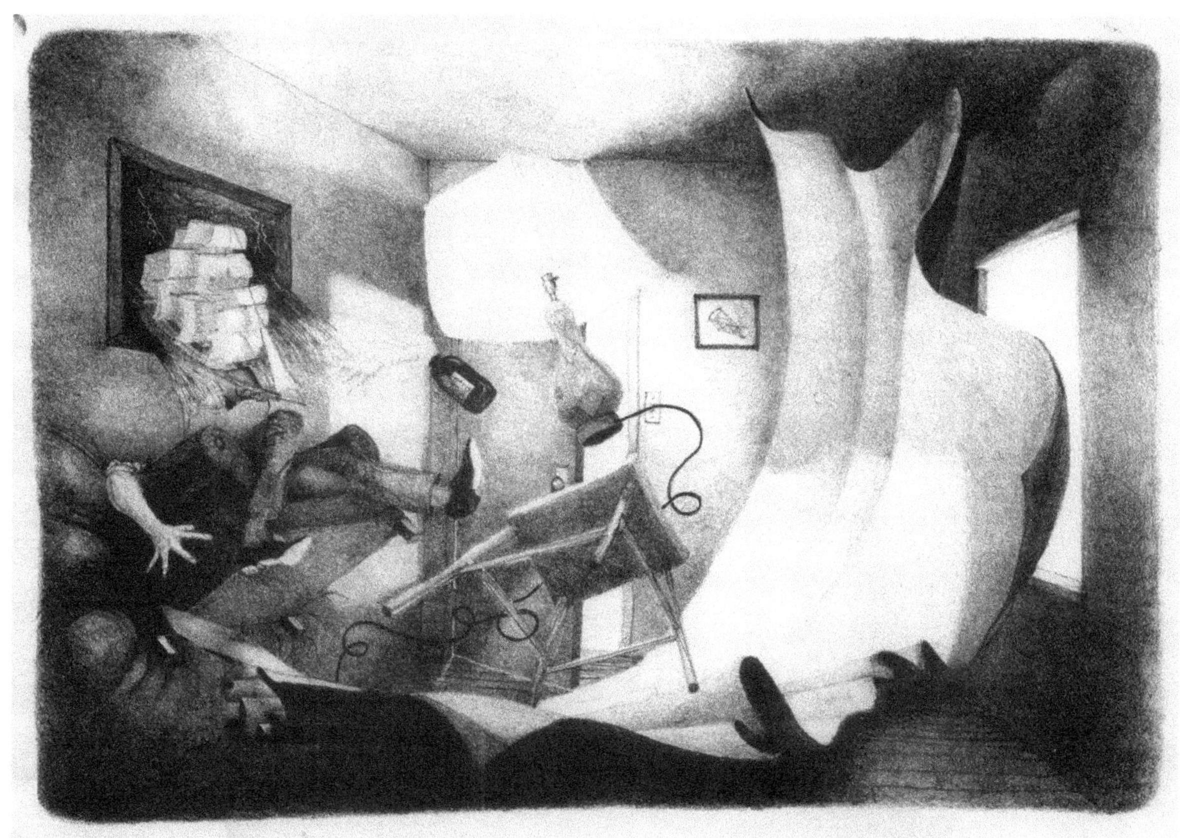

Ink on notebook paper: "Holly"

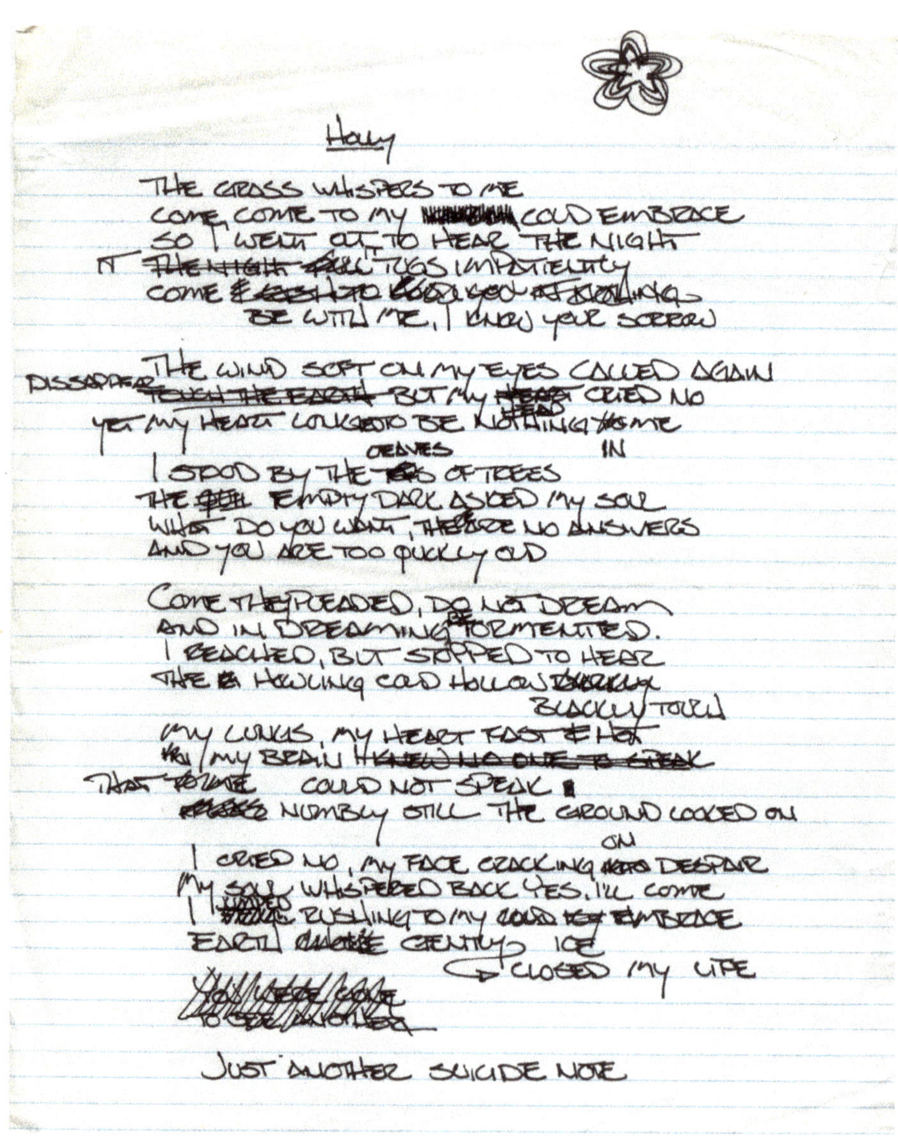

Holly

THE GRASS WHISPERS TO ME
COME, COME TO MY COLD EMBRACE
SO I WENT OUT TO HEAR THE NIGHT
IT TUGS IMPATIENTLY
COME
BE WITH ME, I KNOW YOUR SORROW

THE WIND SOFT ON MY EYES CALLED AGAIN
DISSAPPEAR BUT MY HEAD CRIED NO
YET MY HEART LONGED TO BE NOTHING IN ME

I STOOD BY THE GRAVES OF TREES
THE EMPTY DARK ASKED MY SOUL
WHAT DO YOU WANT, THERE'RE NO ANSWERS
AND YOU ARE TOO QUICKLY OLD

COME THEY PLEADED, DO NOT DREAM
AND IN DREAMING BE TORMENTED.
I REACHED, BUT STOPPED TO HEAR
THE HOWLING COLD HOLLOW BLACKLY TOWN
MY LUNGS, MY HEART FAST & HOT
MY BRAIN
COULD NOT SPEAK
NUMBLY STILL THE GROUND LOOKED ON

I CRIED NO, MY FACE CRACKING ON DESPAIR
MY SOUL WHISPERED BACK YES, I'LL COME
I JUMPED RUSHING TO MY EMBRACE
EARTH GENTLY ICE CLOSED MY LIFE

JUST ANOTHER SUICIDE NOTE

B/W photo, 3.5"x 5.5"

Holly

The grass whispers to me
Come, come to my cold embrace
So I went out to hear the night
It tugs impatiently
Come & be with me, I know your sorrow

The wind soft on my eyes called again
Disappear, but my head cried No
Yet my heart longed to be nothing in me

I stood by the leaves of trees
The empty dark asked my soul
What do you want, There are no answers
And you are too quickly old

Come they pleaded, do not dream
And in dreams be tormented.
I reached, but stopped to hear
The howling cold hollow blackly touch

My lungs, my heart fast & hot
My brain that could not speak.
Numbly still the ground looked on

I cried no, my face cracking on despair
My soul whispered back Yes, I'll come
I jumped rushing to my ice embrace
Earth gently closed my life

Just another suicide note

B/W photo, 3.5"x 5.5"

Paradise and Hell

Two fish in one dream
A dark and brooding stream
Light like eyes, eyes like knives
In this rushing of our lives
The pounding thunder, the roaring splinters
Of this phantom moment
Plunging, tripping, falling, running
Beneath the sound of a scream,
Unheard, unhearable, unbearable dream
Spilling, dropping, never stopping
This darkness, this black and bloody flow
To the sea, the green and salty wonder,
And ocean blue and ocean slow
And ocean grey and ocean vast
An ocean shimmering like the wind
The sliding slipping, slither silver
Swifting seen
Changing changing changing changing
And gone
The fish
S
Are in love

Collage postcard with poem to Holly on back: "Paradise and Hell"

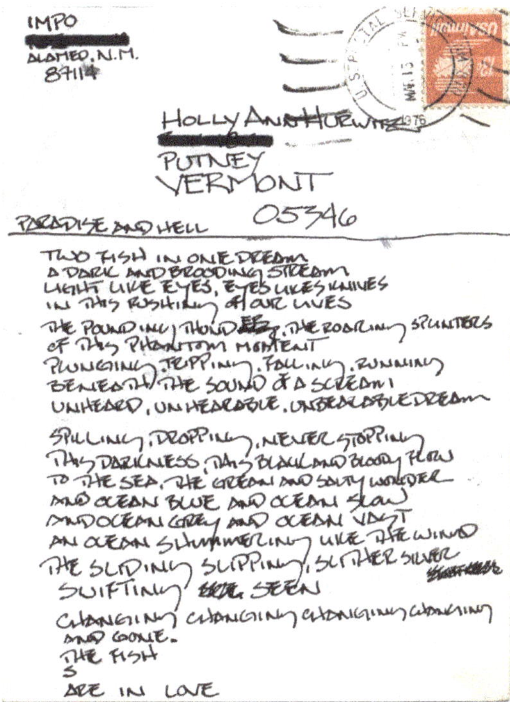

IMPO
ALAMEDA, N.M.
87114

HOLLY ANN HURWITZ
PUTNEY
VERMONT
05346

PARADISE AND HELL

TWO FISH IN ONE DREAM
A DARK AND BROODING STREAM
LIGHT LIKE EYES, EYES LIKES KNIVES
IN THIS RUSHING OF OUR LIVES
THE POUNDING THUNDER, THE ROARING SPLINTERS
OF THIS PHANTOM MOMENT
PLUNGING, TRIPPING, FALLING, RUNNING
BENEATH THE SOUND OF A SCREAM,
UNHEARD, UNHEARABLE, UNBEARABLE DREAM

SPILLING, DROPPING, NEVER STOPPING
THIS DARKNESS, THIS BLACK AND BLOODY FLOW
TO THE SEA, THE GREEN AND SALTY WONDER
AND OCEAN BLUE AND OCEAN SLOW
AND OCEAN GREY AND OCEAN VAST
AN OCEAN SHIMMERING LIKE THE WIND
THE SLIDING SLIPPING, SLITHER SILVER
SWIFTING SEEN
CHANGING CHANGING CHANGING CHANGING
AND GONE.
THE FISHS
ARE IN LOVE

Illustrated Letters to Holly, details.

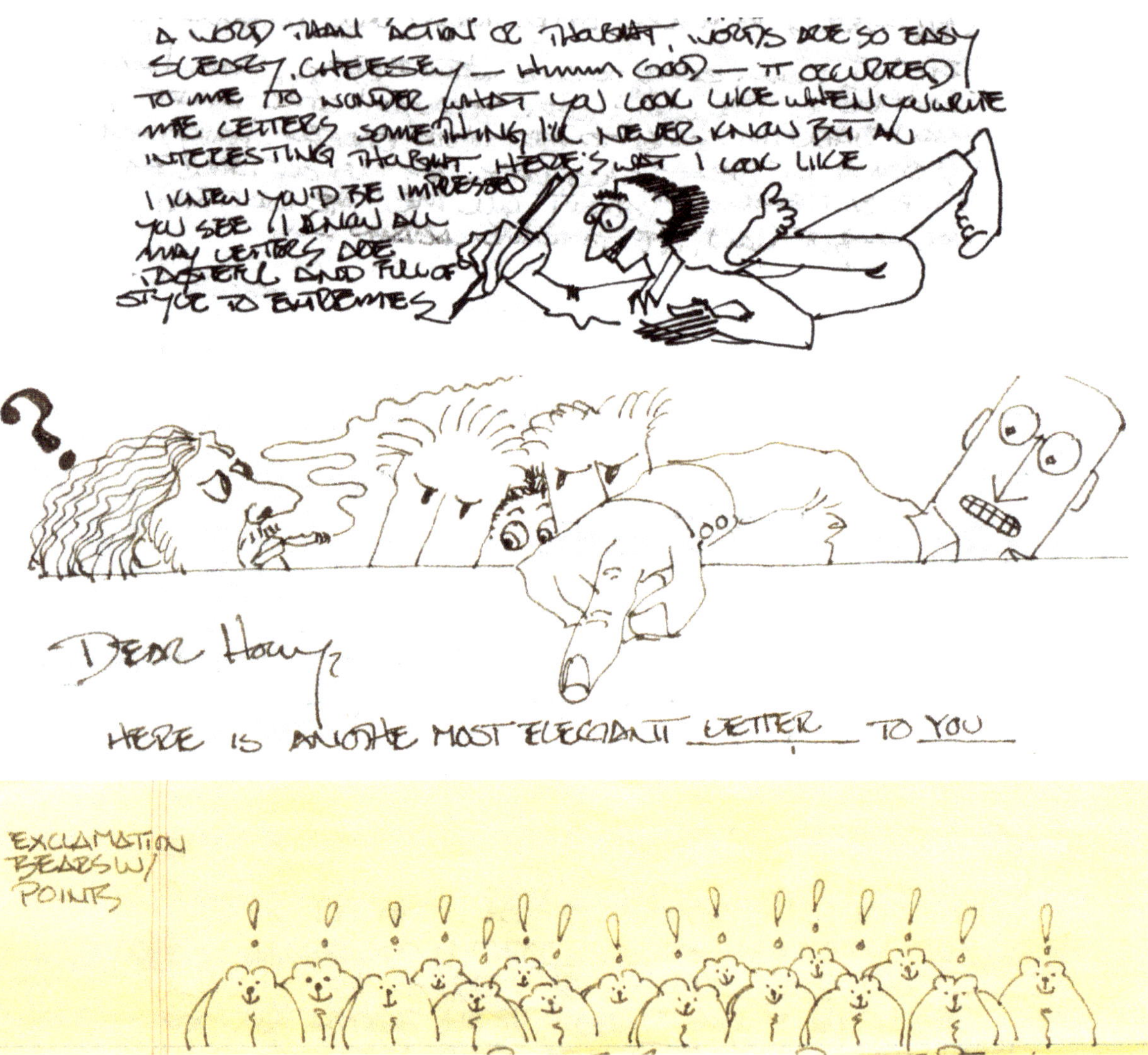

Poem, handwritten on notebook paper; and small ink drawings from sketchbook.

THE MERRY CHASE OF THE BLIND RABBIT AND
THE LEGLESS CLAM.

ON THE SANDS OF OUR DELIGHT
THE SIGHTLESS RABBIT AND CRIPPLED CLAM
RUN WITH THE NIGHT

THE SEA ROLLS IN FOREVER SOON
AND ON THEY SCAMPER WITH THE EYE
UNDER A FALLEN MOON.

RUN ON, RUN ON WHISPERS THE EYE ~~QUICK~~
SO ON THEY TOSS ~~ALL ALONG~~ ALONE
NORTHWARD / ~~[illegible]~~ BY THE SEA.

THE FALLEN, IMMACULATE GULL
SHRIEKS PASSING IN THE WIND
THE BLIND RABBIT AN THE LEGLESS CLAM.

A TUMBLE, JUMBLE VACANT STRAND
~~[illegible]~~ ACCEPTS THEIR SILENT ~~[illegible]~~ JOY

MOON FEMALE GULL-MALE

UNDER A FALLEN, SILVER MOON MADE OF ASH,
BY THE ~~ENDLESS~~ VACANT SEA, IN A ~~THE~~ TRANQUIL NIGHT,
OVER THE SANDS OF OUR DELIGHT THEY FLASH.
THE BLIND RABBIT AND THE LEGLESS CLAM

THEY SCAMPER ON IN A SEPARATE FLIGHT,
~~WATCHED~~ SEEN BY A FALLING, IMMACULATE GULL.
LOST ALONG THE STRAND, RUNNING WITHOUT SIGHT.
THE RABBIT FOLLOWS WHAT DOES NOT MOVE

Letter to Holly, 6"x 9"

THE FLOWERS ARE FROM THE MOUNTAINS. LOVE, VAN

Etching, 11"x 9.75

Etching, 7.75"x 4.75"

Ink on paper, 11"x 14"

Ink on board, with next page, 20"x 6"

Ink on board.

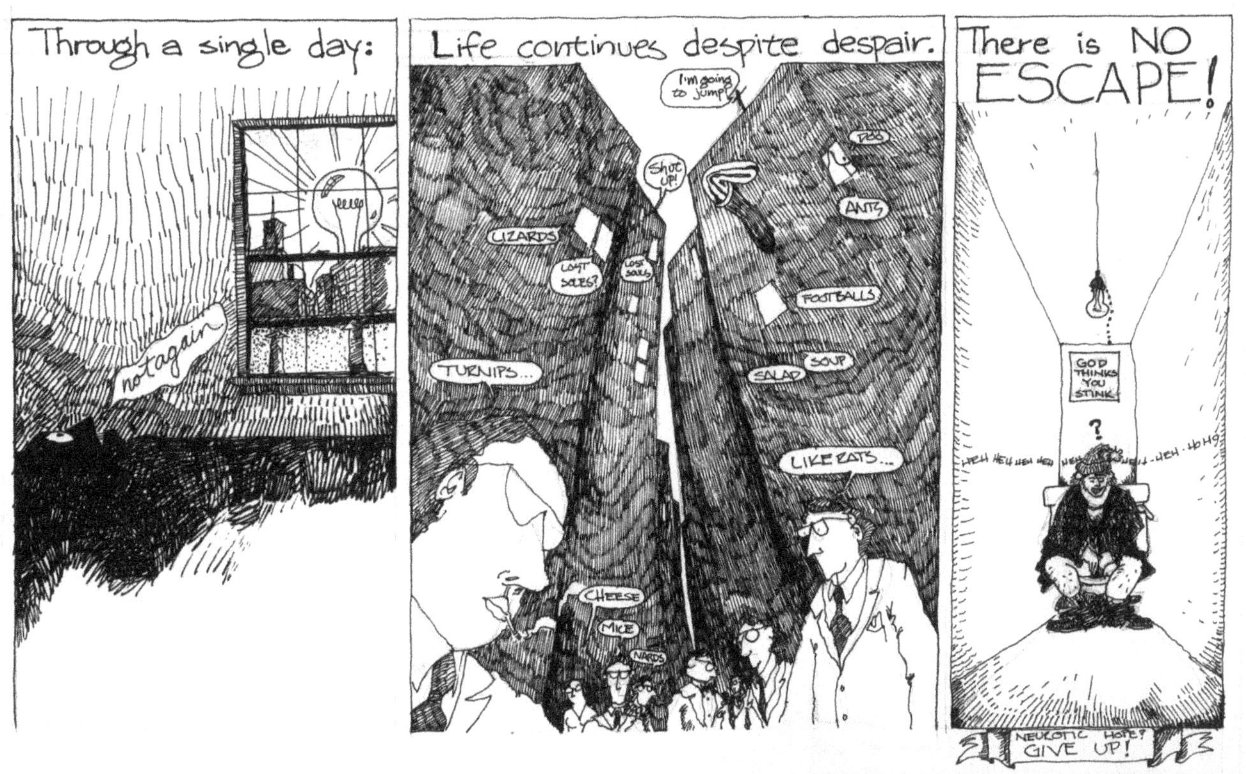
Through a single day:
notagain
Life continues despite despair.
I'm going to jump!
Shut up!
POO
ANTS
LIZARDS
LOST SOLES?
LOST SOULS
FOOTBALLS
TURNIPS...
SOUP
SALAD
LIKE RATS...
CHEESE
MICE
NARDS
There is NO ESCAPE!
GOD THINKS YOU STINK
?
NEUROTIC HOPE? GIVE UP!

Letter excerpt, handwritten: “Back to the strangeness”

(2)

BACK TO THE STRANGENESS OF LIFE. IT LIES IN THE EXPERIENCE OF EVENTS WHICH ARE FAMILIAR BUT WITHOUT ANY INTRINSIC MEANING OR WORTH, THUS EMPTY, OR HOLLOW— JUST LIKE MY JOB, EVEN THE ONE AT THE RESTUARANT IS ONLY A LITTLE BETTER. PERHAPS I LIKE ART ONLY IN THAT IT IS MORE PERSONALLY SATISFYING, BUT AS FOR DOING IT FOR OTHER PEOPLE, I'M NOT TOO SURE. IT MAY BE I DON'T HAVE THE GALL TO ASSUME MY WORK IS EARTH-SHATTERING. THIS I DOUBT. IN FACT THERE IS VERY LITTLE I DO I CONSIDER TO BE WORTH THE TIME I WASTE ON IT. THE ONLY THING ABOUT ART IS I'M IN CONTROL, IN SOME SENSE, OF MY OWN TIME & MY WORK. SO, IN THAT RESPECT I ENJOY IT. I'M NOT TRYING TO PLEASE ANYBODY, OR RATHER I AM, AS I LIKE THE THINGS I DO TO ENTERTAIN IN SOME WAY. THE TROUBLE WITH BEING INTELLIGENT IN WHATEVER CAPACITY IS THAT ONE CANNOT ESCAPE ITS CURSE, WHICH IS THINKING. TRAINED OR NOT, A MIND WILL CONTINUE TO FUNCTION DESPITE ATTEMPTS TO AVOID IT. AH. SWEET MOTIVATION— THAT TERRIBLE ANGEL, ETC. CONSISTENT FOLLY IS ITS OWN REWARD, OR SOMETHING.

Ink drawing from 11"x 14" sketchbook.

Back to the strangeness of life. It lies in the experience of events which are familiar but without any intrinsic meaning or worth, thus empty, or hollow—Just like my job, and even the one at the Restaurant is only a little better. Perhaps I like art only in that it is more personally satisfying, but as for doing it for other people, I'm not too sure. It may be I don't have the gall to assume my work is earth-shattering. This I doubt. In fact there is very little I do consider to be worth the time I waste on it. The only thing about art is I'm in control. In some sense, of my own time & my work. So in that respect I enjoy it. I'm not trying to please anybody, or rather I am, as I like the things I do to entertain in some way. The trouble with being intelligent in whatever capacity is that one cannot escape its curse. Which is thinking trained or not, a mind will continue to function—Despite attempts to avoid it. Ah. Sweet motivation—that terrible Angel. Etc. Consistent folly is its Own reward, or something.

11"x 14" sketchbook, front and back covers.

Ink drawing from 11"x 14" sketchbook.

Ink drawing from 11"x 14" sketchbook.

Ink drawing from 11”x 14” sketchbook.

Ink drawing from 11"x 14" sketchbook.

Ink drawings from 11"x 14" sketchbook.

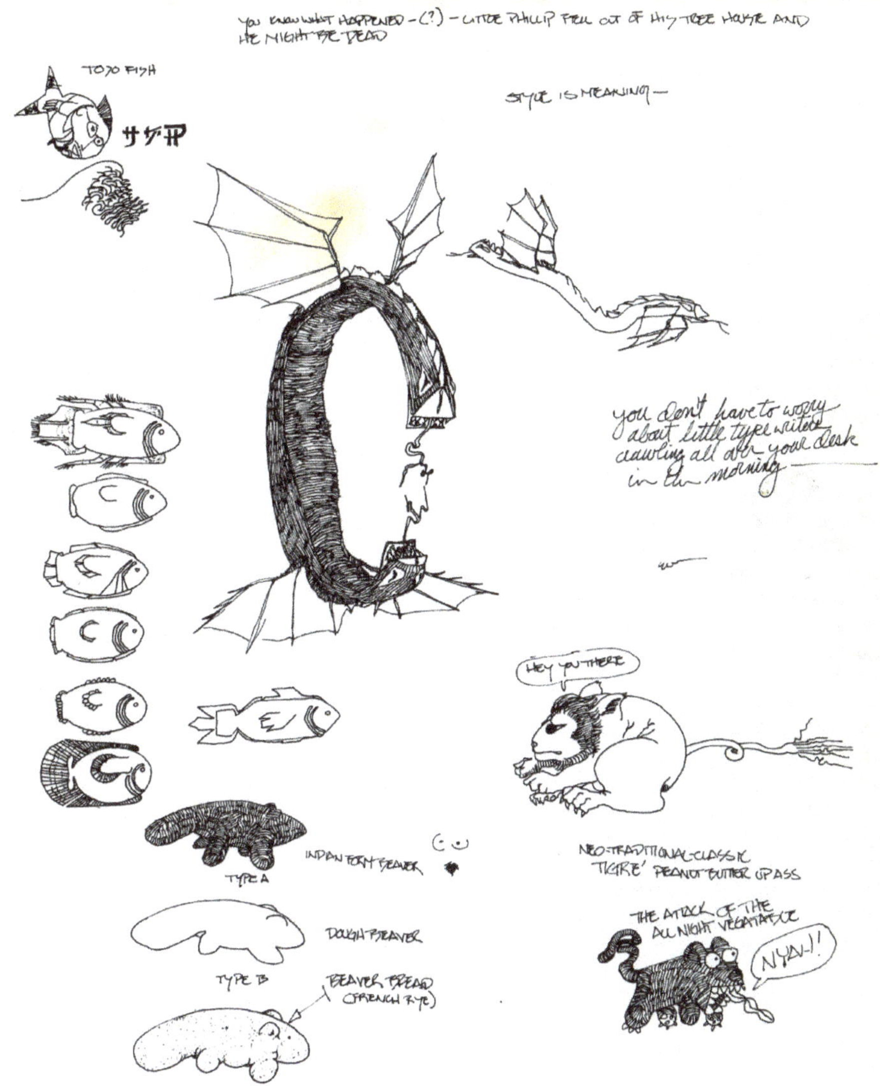

Small pencil sketches in 12"x 18" pad.

Charcoal sketches on newsprint, 10"x 8", signed 1/10/75, Van Hooker, with titles (clockwise from top left): Blueberry, Apple ala Mode, Pecan, Coconut Cream.

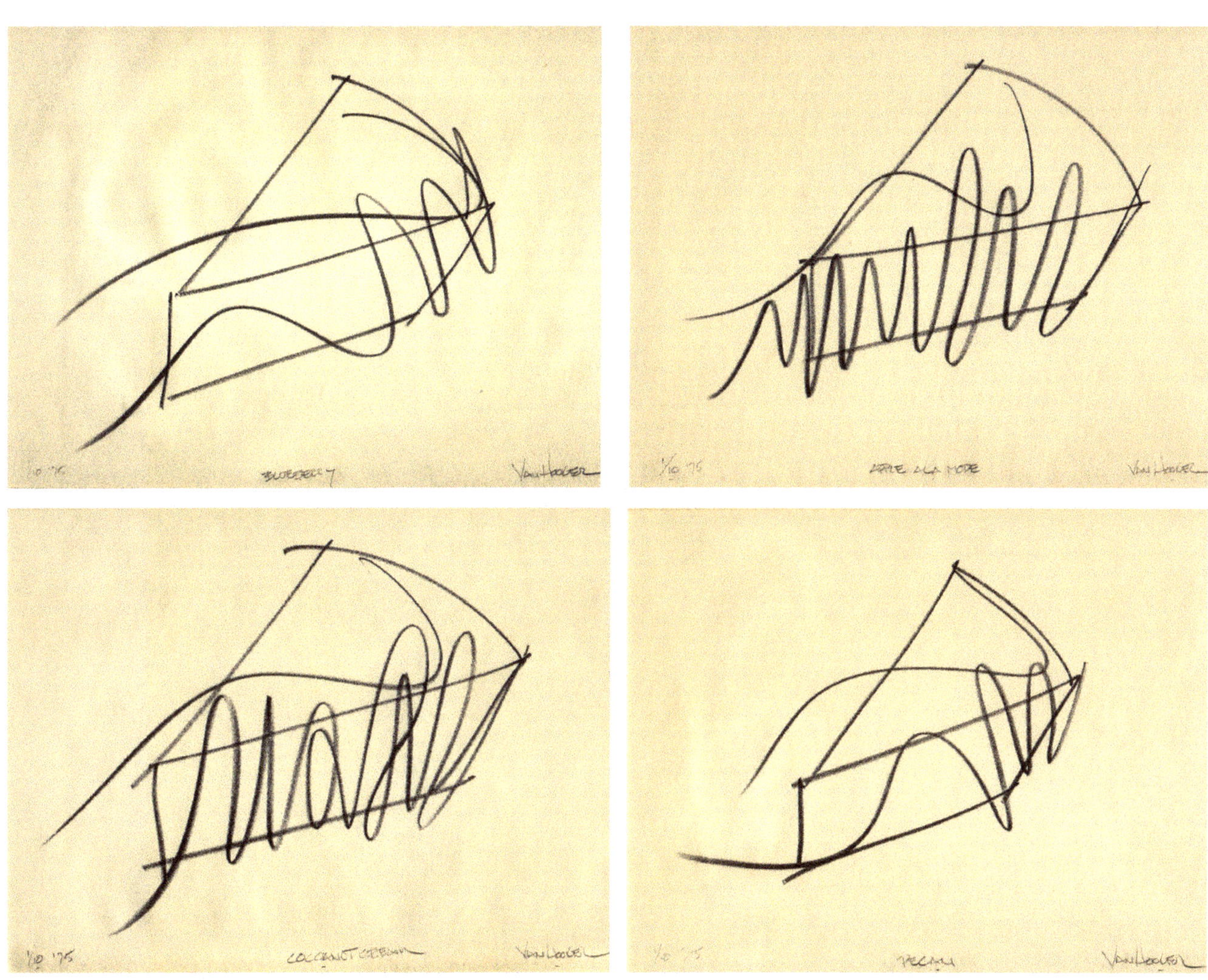

Ink sketches in 12"x 18" pad.

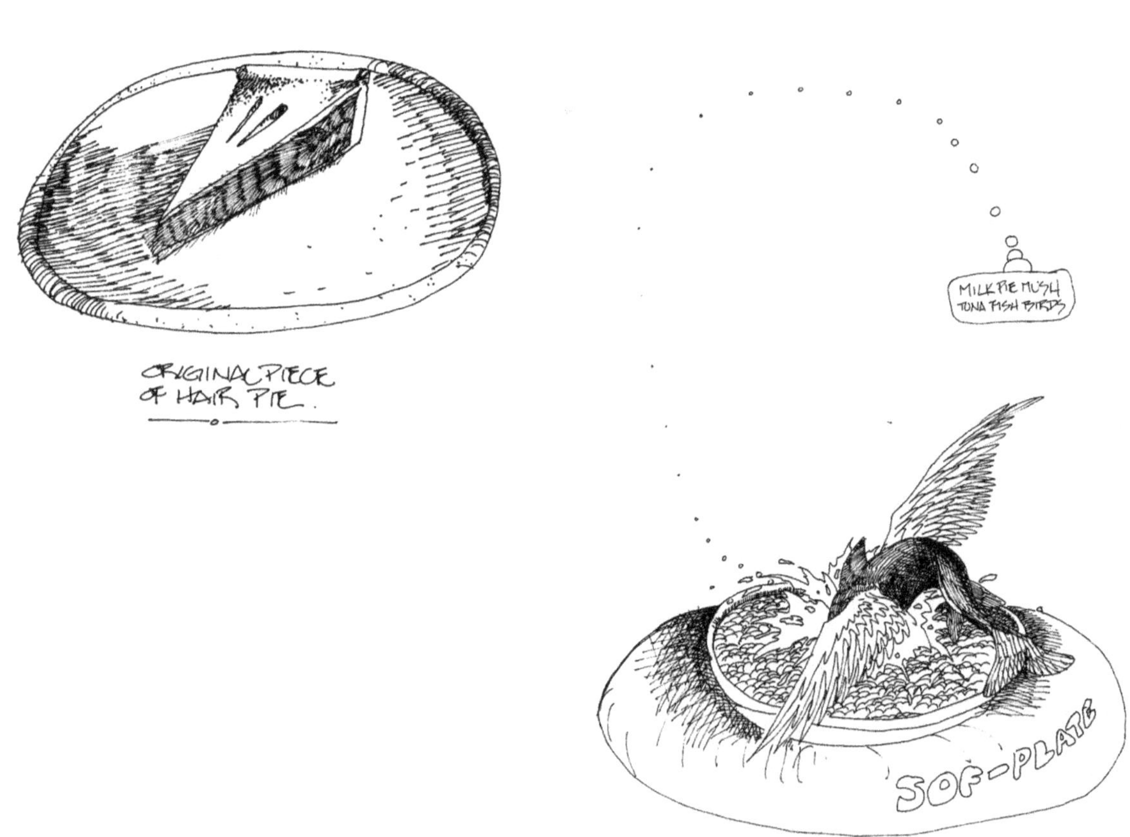

Ink drawings in 11"x 14" pad.

Pencil sketches in 11"x 14" pad.

Etching, Pie, 8"x 10"

Etching, Pie 2, 8”x 10”

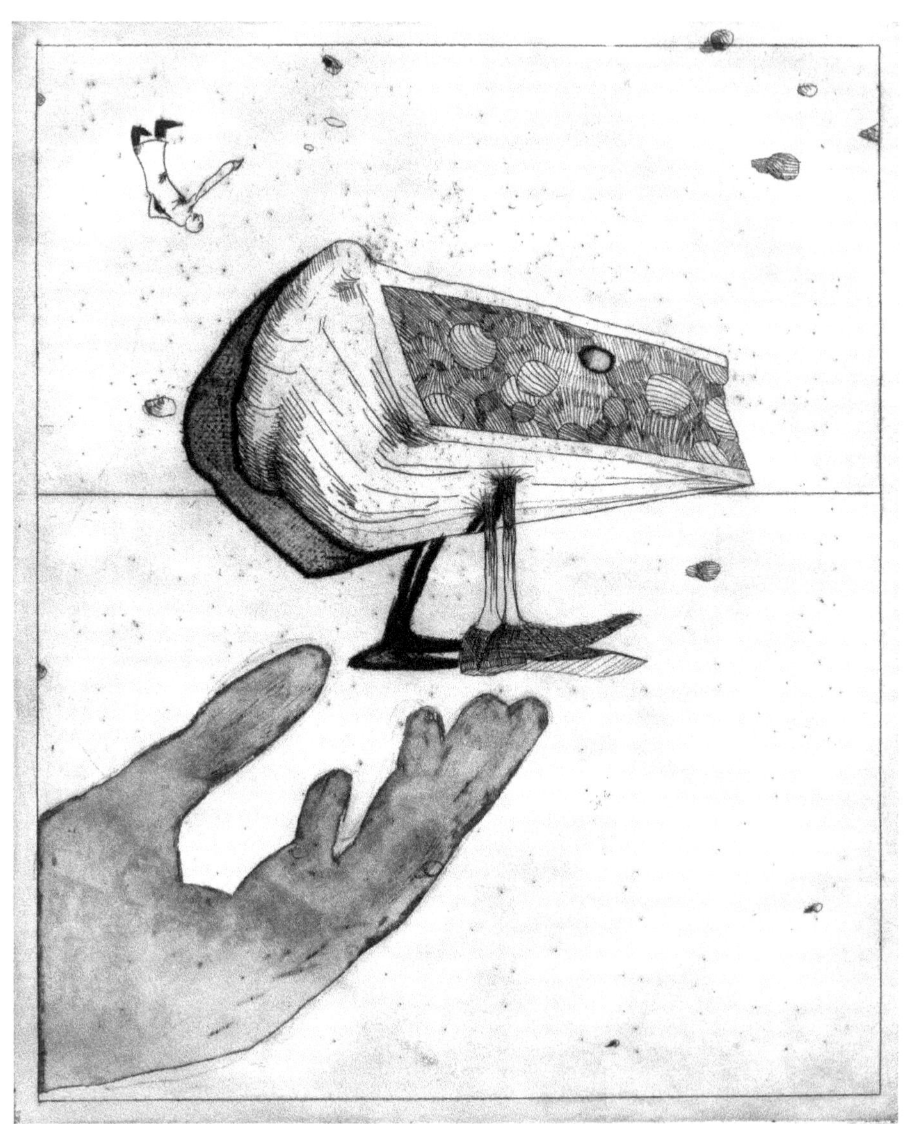

Etching, Pie 3, 8"x 10"

Etching, Pie 4, 8"x 10"

Ink on notebook paper.

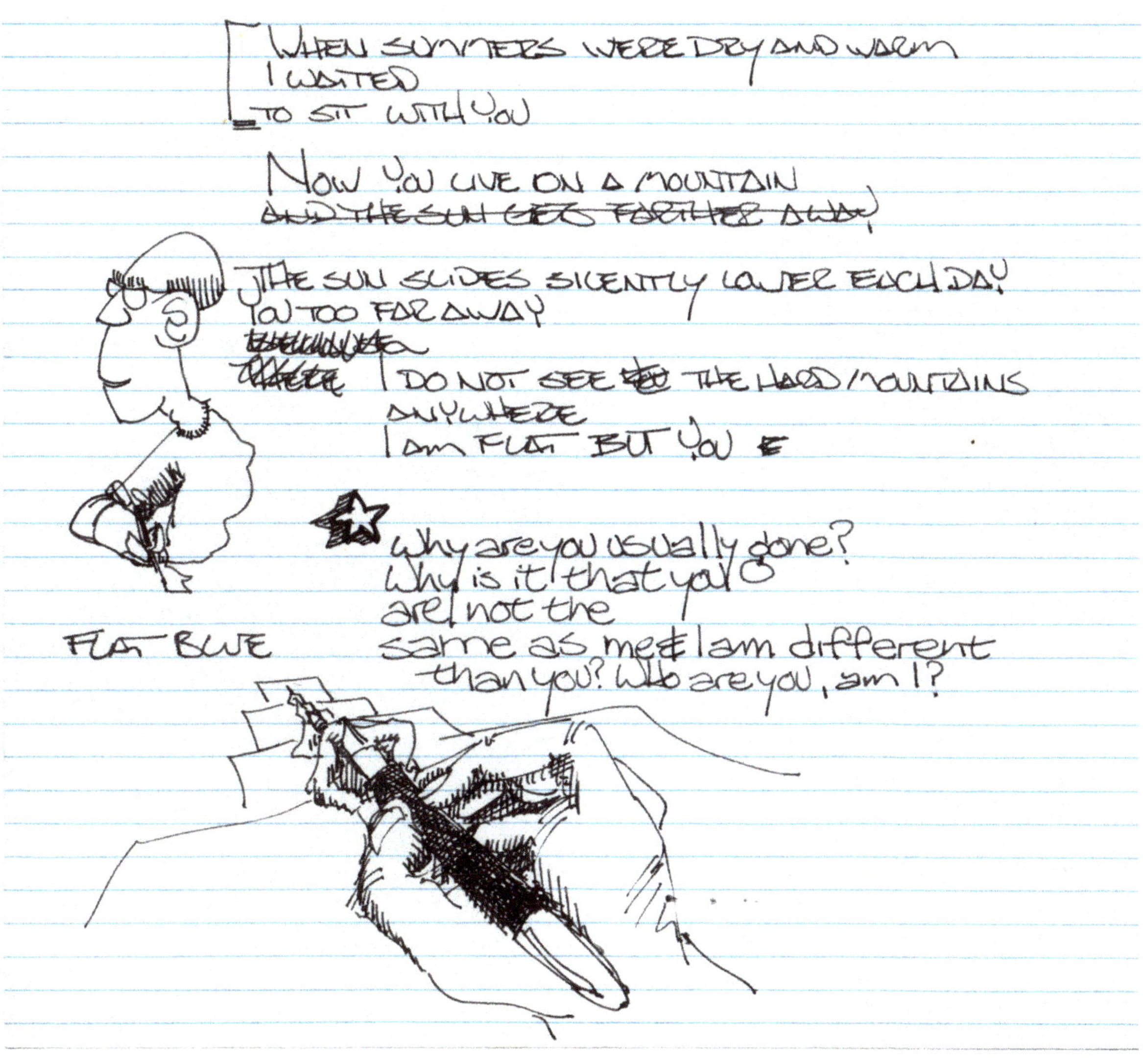

Photo self-portrait (b/w 6"x 4.5"): A photo Van took of himself in Kansas City. He liked it. He didn't Smoke. The cigarette was a prop. —HH

Lithograph, 8”x 10”, German translation by Franz Vote.

Du gehst mich auf dem
Bürgersteig vorbei
aber verstehst nicht
das ich lächeln könnte

Flüchtene[n] Augen (flüchtene)
voll mit Fürcht
und Hoffnung
Wir sind vorbei
Ich verschwinde
du sicher bist
eine störende Phantasie

Aber ich lebe
Und du traumst nicht (träumst)

You walk toward me on the
sidewalk
but you don’t understand
that I could smile

Fleeting eyes
full of fear
and hope
we’ve passed by each other
I disappear
you are most certainly
a disturbing fantasy

Yet I live
and you do not dream

Ink on notebook paper.

And in the end,
All the love that
Is within needs
To be told, otherwise
No one will
Ever know that
They were ever
Loved. The distance
Is already
Too great, so why
Is it, we try
To make it greater

REMEMBERING CHIP

VAN DORN HOOKER, III

Van Dorn Hooker, III ("Chip") Biographical Notes

9/15/54, born in Santa Fe, New Mexico at St. Vincent's Hospital
10/12/76, died in motorcycle accident in Portland, Oregon
Parents: Van Dorn Hooker, Jr. and Marjorie (Peggy) Mead (d. 11/11/86)
Siblings: Ann Clarke and John H. Hooker

Education:

Wood-Gormley elementary school in Santa Fe
May, 1972, graduated Albuquerque Academy
Dec. 1972, received a Culinary Certificate from Albuquerque Technical Vocational Institute
Sept. 1973–May 1974, attended Earlham College in Richmond, IN
Sept. 1974–May 1976, attended Kansas City Art Institute
Fall, 1976, accepted to Brown University and was preparing to transfer there in the spring of 1977 to pursue more literary interests

Special honors and awards, clubs, teams, organizations while at Albuquerque Academy:

Member of soccer team 1971 and 1972, lettered in soccer
Senior Class Fine Arts Award 1972

After Chip's death, the family established the Van Dorn Hooker, III Memorial Fund at the Albuquerque Academy, out of which awards are given to promising art students.

Opposite page: Baby picture; Boyhood picture; High school photo; all provided by VDH.

My Son, Chip

I suppose one way to start would be to say that Chip saved my life. You see, one night after dinner I was smoking, and he asked me why I smoked. And I said, 'Well, I enjoy it, I like it and it tastes good,' and he said, 'Well, I'll make you a deal, if you quit smoking, I'll never smoke.' And that was the last cigarette I ever smoked, and I'm ninety-two years old now. I can imagine that I have Chip to thank for a lot of those years.

My father was Van Dorn Hooker and I'm Van Dorn Jr. So my first son was Van Dorn Hooker, III. I gave him the nickname Chip because Van Dorn is a hard name to carry, but I did want to carry it on because it has meant a great deal to me. 'Chip off the old block' is where it came from. His friends called him Van.

Chip was born in Santa Fe, and early on we realized that he had a fantastic ability to read. I have a photograph of him lying in bed with a bottle of milk, the nipple in his mouth, reading. He couldn't have been over a year and a half or two years old. He became an avid reader, and he collected many, many books. He had a tremendous mind and we cultivated it as much as possible.

He became quite a skilled artist on his own. He loved to draw, did a lot of drawings while at the Albuquerque Academy. He took an art course under Mike O'Connor, who thought he was very talented, and a good calligrapher. He did a lot of cartoons, many of them reflected his attitude on life. His cartoons have a sort of a whimsical touch to them, he had a good sense of humor and a great potential as an artist. But rather than pursuing an art career he had decided to go to Brown University and major in English literature.

His writings reflected a deep understanding early on of life. It showed a certain questioning on his part, almost a sadness with the world. The first time I ran across his writings, I was a little upset by the melancholy aspect of them—the sadness that he showed. Why was he sad? I don't think I ever asked him. I would like people to know a little bit about what a very fine person he was, and to maybe gain some thoughts from what he wrote. A lot of remarkable writings for a teenager. I think it was just his personality. I don't know how much influence his mother and I had on him, though his mother was a wonderful person, very beautiful and intelligent.

Chip was an outstanding student and a great soccer player. The soccer coach mentioned that he was one of the best high school soccer players he had ever coached. Chip didn't know what he wanted to do. The first thing he did when he graduated from the Academy was to take a course in the culinary arts from a vocational school here in Albuquerque. He became a cook, first in a Walgreen's store serving hot dogs, but later he worked in the restaurant on Sandia Peak. He never stayed with a restaurant very long. He went with a restaurant here in Corrales. I remember one night he served a special dinner for his mother and me there. He was a very kind, thoughtful person.

Van's photo collage portrait of his father (b/w 5.5"x6.75").

He got the idea that he would go to college, and he picked Earlham College in Richmond, Indiana. He fell in love with a young lady named Holly he met there. He went to Earlham for one year, but he was very unhappy with the art program, so he transferred to the Kansas City Art Institute. He went there about a year, but was unhappy with the curriculum because it didn't teach the fine arts but taught students how to become commercial artists.

He earned enough money to buy a very used Studebaker, which he drove. And he later bought a motorcycle, but he knew that I had a fear of him having a motorcycle. I would never have found out about it, because he left the motorcycle at a friend's house, but I got a call from an insurance agent wanting my signature on the insurance policy on the motorcycle because he was not 21. Not long after that, Chip applied to Brown University and was accepted, but he had to wait for the beginning of the spring semester, so he and Holly decided to bike to California by way of Albuquerque. By that time he had acquired his motorcycle. They went on to Portland Oregon, where his sister was working, and one day he and Holly went over to Riverside, sort of a resort town west of Portland, near the Pacific Ocean. Then, on the way back, a truck made a left turn and struck them, and he was killed. Holly was hurt, seriously injured, but she recovered.

Something happened to me. I was standing on the porch, talking to Holly's father who had come here for the memorial service. A bird landed on my hand. I found out that it was a Creeper—they come through, migrating, but I have never seen one before or since. What did it mean? I like to think it was a sign from or a symbol of Chip.

I would have hoped that whatever Chip decided to do would have made him happy, and that he would enjoy life. Whether he became an artist, I wanted him to be a great artist and do good work. If he decided to be an English literature professor I would want him to be a good one. He had such potential.

—Van Dorn Hooker, Jr.

Bird on Van Dorn Jr.'s hand, November 1976, detail.

Father's Day drawing by Chip, date unknown, 8.5"x11", marker on paper.

Ann Remembers

My younger brother Chip was a delight to know. My fondest memory of him is as a pre-teen. At the dinner table, he and our younger brother John would make impersonations and be generally very silly, I would laugh so hard my sides would hurt and my eyes would tear. As another mother said to me a generation later about my son and his friend, who were of a similar age and very silly, "silly boys are wonderful."

It is with mixed feelings that I write this remembrance. The last time I saw Chip was as I stepped off the bus we were on in Portland, Oregon. I don't remember where we had been. All I remember is saying goodbye, not knowing that I would never see him again. We were just beginning to become reacquainted as young adults when he died. As a teen, Chip became immersed in the demands of the Albuquerque Academy and I left for college. He visited me once and we corresponded from time to time. His letters were very thoughtful and expressed a lament that we did not know each other very well. To his credit, after I had finished graduate school and was working in Portland, Oregon, he and his girlfriend Holly rode a motorcycle from New Mexico to California and up the coast to Oregon to visit Holly's sister at Reed College and me. Chip wanted to get to know me better, and Holly wanted to see her sister for a few months before they moved to Providence, Rhode Island. Chip had been admitted to Brown University, and we were very happy for that, as he was so gifted.

From left: John, Ann, Van; photo provided by VDH.

From left: Ann, Van, John, Peggy; photo provided by VDH.

Chip and Ann; photo provided by AHC.

Chip, to me, is, thus, forever young, and I am exquisitely aware of the fragility of life and the need to be grateful for every moment. After losing Chip so suddenly, I told my son every day as he was growing up that I love him. My son, now in the contemporary art auction business in London, has said he wishes he had known his Uncle Chip, and feels he would have enjoyed knowing him. I likewise believe I was fortunate to have known Chip.

The night Chip died, I was watching the stars. I do believe that we are made of stardust and that when we look at the stars, we can see Chip drawing silly cartoons with stardust. To quote from Antoine de Saint-Exupéry's *The Little Prince,* which our father greatly admired: "You—you alone will have the stars as no one else has them... In one of the stars I shall be living. In one of them I shall be laughing. And so it will be as if all the stars were laughing, when you look at the sky at night... You—only you—will have stars that can laugh." (Antoine de Saint-Exupéry, *El Principito)*

—Ann H. Clarke

Mother's Day drawing by Chip, date unknown, 11"x 8.5", marker on paper.

John Remembers

It was fun growing up with my older brother, Chip. I admired him greatly for most of my young life, and I envied his artistic talent. Tried to copy him in many ways, but also tried to hide the fact that I was copying him. Of course, as an older brother, he knew how to torment me—just enough to make me angry, but not so much as to get into trouble with our parents. We moved to Corrales, New Mexico when I was eight and he was ten. There weren't many other children nearby to play with.

Chip and John, photo provided by VDH.

We played many games together, like "crab soccer" which apparently has become more common today. We played pick-up games of baseball with a couple of other boys in an alfalfa field that is now another house lot, and some "touch football" at a nearby neighbor's house in their little grass yard. One particular game is memorable for the pile-on that resulted in my going to the ER with a broken arm.

I realize now that all of us who knew Chip knew a different person. My mother and father each saw him through their love, experience and age. My sister knew him as her silly younger brother. I knew him as my clever and bigger older brother. We joked around a lot. I didn't understand his darker moods, but he had a wicked sense of humor about school and life. He was sour about his high school years, a non-conformist. Some of his cartoons from that time lampooned the school and especially football players. He and I played high school soccer, but he was always the better athlete.

From left: Peggy, Chip, Van Dorn, Ann, John; Peggy's mother seated in front; photo provided by VDH.

He had a dark view of society of the early 1970s. He mocked the conventional world. He and I enjoyed watching Star Trek and a satirical public television series of the time, "The Great American Dream Machine." This was before Monty Python. Chip was a dreamer and an idealist.

Chip's work echoed some of the satirical cartoonists and pop artists gaining notice at the time, like Robert Crumb, Peter Max and Ralph Steadman. Perhaps he once dreamed of joining their ranks, though he became more interested in fine art and literature as he went along. Chip had so much talent, but if I were asked what his future would be, I could not imagine it.

That summer of 1976 was the last time I saw and spoke with Chip at our parents' house in Corrales, NM. We had gone for a drive and talked in the car. It was the first and last conversation we had as two young adults. I enjoyed Chip immensely for the years I knew him. He didn't know it, but he was my playmate, guide and mentor. I miss him terribly and wish I could talk to him today.

—John Hooker

Holly Remembers

I have been looking through boxes that contain everything I have that belonged to Van: lots of letters covered with drawings, cartoons, pages and pages of written work, finished art work from his time at Kansas City Art Institute. I want to write something that is alive and joyful, something that captures even a tiny momentary glimmer of him. Because those boxes exude life—a passionate, searching, creative engagement with the world.

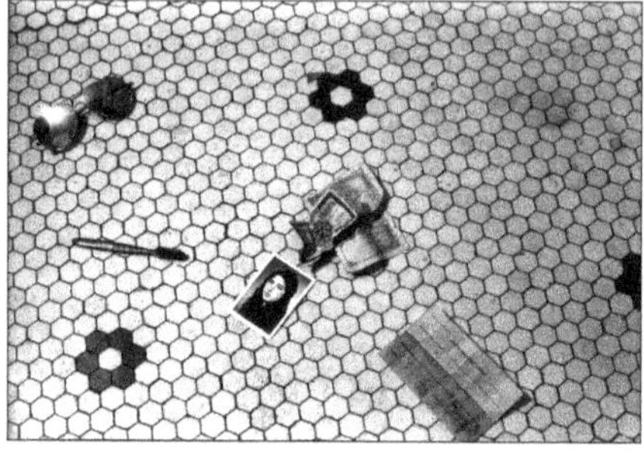

Van's photo collage portrait of Holly (b/w 5.75"x4").

Experiencing and creating art seemed to provide Van with a way of seeing and expressing himself in relation to the world; a vehicle to search for truth and meaning, and even beauty, in a world full of superficiality, pain, and suffering. He was as exquisitely sensitive to that pain as he was truly sustained by the deep emotional connections with those he loved, by the beauty in the natural world, and by the transcendent power of art.

Art, in any form, is what he responded to in the world. He had an insatiable curiosity to experience art in many forms—film, photography, music, literature, as well as graphic art.

He had an equal drive to create—it wasn't what he did, it was who he was. His written work was often dark, full of angst and despair at what he saw in the world, and the sense of alienation he felt. But, his drawings especially were also humerous and hopeful. It was all an expression of his truth, a genuine, undiluted, creative representation of his singularly unique self. There was no barrier between his vast intellect, his creativity, his physical self, his soul, and the nib of his pen. I feel his vital living presence in those ink drawings—they are everywhere—in the margins of letters, on the backs of envelopes, in scraps of paper—on anything that was near him when a spark of creativity or an idea hit him. They flowed out of him and onto the paper without thought or hesitation, his rapt attention focused on the line of black ink transforming itself into an expression/creation both deeply personal, and transcendent—a reflection of him, but so much more.

I am so glad I knew him. When I see those drawings, he is with me.

—Holly Hurwitz

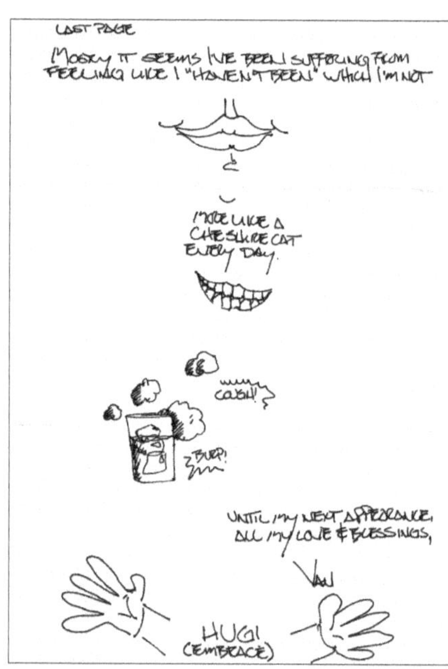

LAST PAGE

MOSTLY IT SEEMS I'VE BEEN SUFFERING FROM FEELING LIKE I "HAVEN'T BEEN" WHICH I'M NOT

I'M MORE LIKE A CHESHIRE CAT EVERY DAY.

COUGH!

BURP!

UNTIL MY NEXT APPEARANCE, ALL MY LOVE & BLESSINGS,

VAN

HUG! (EMBRACE)

Note to Holly.

Acknowledgments

This collection has been published at the behest of Van Dorn Hooker, Jr. from photos, artwork, letters and notes in his possession and loaned by Ann Clarke, John Hooker and Holly Hurwitz. Also instrumental in the preparation of the book were Claiborne (Mike) O'Connor, who first undertook the process of gathering and sorting the artwork; Ashley Jordan, who assisted with the texts; Franz Vote who provided the German translation; Zelda Leah Gatuskin, designer and editor, and Jim Smith and his staff at Sunstone Press.

www.ingramcontent.com/pod-product-compliance
Lightning Source LLC
Chambersburg PA
CBHW042046030726
47599CB00019B/2388

* 9 7 8 1 6 3 2 9 3 0 3 1 6 *